52 Weekends in Connecticut

Lake Compounce Family Theme Park is the oldest amusement park in the country.

52 Weekends in Connecticut

Day Trips & Easy Getaways from the Litchfield Hills to Long Island Sound

ANDI MARIE CANTELE

THE COUNTRYMAN PRESS

WOODSTOCK, VERMONT

We welcome your comments and suggestions. Please contact Editor, The Countryman Press, P.O. Box 748, Woodstock, Vermont 05091, or e-mail countrymanpress@wwnorton.com.

First Edition

ISBN 978-0-88150-721-8

Book design and composition by Dawn DeVries Sokol
Cover photograph © Jack McConnell, www.mcconnellpix.com,
Courtesy Mystic Seaport, www.mysticseaport.org
Maps by Paul Woodward, © The Countryman Press

Published by The Countryman Press, P.O. Box 748, Woodstock, VT 05091

Distributed by W. W. Norton & Company, Inc., 500 Fifth Avenue, New York, NY 10110

Printed in the United States of America

10 9 8 7 6 5 4 3 2 1

TO CECIL

CONTENTS

Summer

Fall

Winter

ACKNOWLEDGMENTS

THANKS TO THE STAFF at the Countryman Press, especially Jennifer Thompson, Kermit Hummel, Glenn Novak, Fred Lee, and Kelly Thompson, whose vision, expertise, and support made this book possible.

Thanks also to Bob Dowling, Mike O'Farrell, Jessica Summers, David Holahan, Audrey Babbitt, Tammi Flynn, Paula Bender, Tracey Blackman, Marcia Powell, Augusta Girard, Patti Philippon, Hedy Barton, Robyn Rifkin, Cathy Hagadorn, Tim Gagne, Kelley Citroni, Wayne Mattox, Mary Ellen White, Paul Marte, Laura Soll, Janet Roberts, Helen Kauder, Allen Cockerline, Alicia Wayland, Sally Whipple, Louise DeMars, Ralph Harris, Bob Milne, Jim Nelson, Steve Ardussi, and Nancy Spitzer. They are among the countless individuals who were generous with their time, ideas, and advice, going out of their way to get whatever information I needed or connect me with people to interview. Still others—lobstermen, balloon pilots, highland dancers, museum docents, and musicians, to name a few—provided the personal stories and insider tips that color a travel guide.

I am also grateful to Johannes Neuer, T. Charles Erickson, Chris Rutsch, Cory Mazon, Jennifer Wolinski, Michael Marsland, Mark LaMonica, Robert Gregson, Melanie Brigockas, Mark Yuknat, Jerry Hyres, Renea Topp, and Marla Patterson, who provided beautiful images for use in many of the chapters.

Thanks are also due to Lisa Hodkoski, Jean Fusco, Janet and Wayne Waldron, Deb and George Roberts, and Felicia Carucci for accompanying me on journeys around the state. Finally, I am grateful to my family for their enthusiasm and support, and, especially, to Brian, whose company made my travels around Connecticut more fun than work.

INTRODUCTION

READY FOR A LITTLE TIME OFF? Here's the first thing a first-time visitor to Connecticut needs to know: Small is beautiful, and a weekend is perfect for a spin through this little state that delivers big on year-round fun. Every weekend you're not exploring is an opportunity missed, so to get you going, I searched Connecticut to find fabulous getaway spots, then handpicked 52 destinations, from my own must-do trips in my home state to hidden jewels I discovered along the way, to bring you in and show you around New England's southernmost state.

Thanks to its diminutive size—just 100 miles across and less than 60 miles top to bottom—Connecticut is easily traveled; no place in the nation's third-smallest state is more than a three-hour drive from any other. Nevertheless, there's much to see and do. In fact, few places compact so much variety in so little space. It's all here: the cosmopolitan Gold Coast, the rural Quiet Corner, the sophistication and natural beauty of the Litchfield Hills, and the historic and lovely Connecticut River valley and shoreline along Long Island Sound.

This is a definitive guide to all that Connecticut has to offer the weekend traveler, full of insider tips on where to go and what to see throughout the seasons. It includes, naturally, the state's most famous landmarks (Mystic Seaport, Gillette Castle, Wadsworth Atheneum), and all are worth a visit. But find its best-kept secrets (historic gardens, ski jumps, seal-watching cruises) and you have a look at the real Connecticut, the kind of trips where visitors leave with a sense of place.

Connecticut treasures its past, which is shaped as much by its maritime history as by a rich agricultural heritage. It's a state brimming with things old and charming, from stately village greens and historic country inns to vintage whaling ships and clapboard farmhouses built by New

England's earliest settlers. Like the seasons, Connecticut's landscape has many moods. Nearly two-thirds of the state is covered in forested hills, rolling farmland, and state parks. The Appalachian Trail wends its way through, as does New England's longest river and miles of quiet back roads, offering postcard pinups at every turn. Throw in literally hundreds of festivals and events taking place all year long, and there's something suited to most every taste.

Connecticut is also the closest New England state to New York City and points south, which may explain why so many visitors find it the ideal destination for getting away without going far away. Consider this: More and more time-pressed travelers are favoring quick weekend getaways over traditional weeklong trips, according to the Travel Industry Association of America, a group that monitors travel trends. With gasoline prices soaring and vacation time shrinking, here's a state to explore in a couple days from top to bottom, with not a lot of driving in between. Good things come in small packages, goes the old adage, and in Connecticut, small has its advantages.

So go out and explore, and hit the roads less traveled along the way. If you see one that looks interesting, take it; if you pass a shop that appears unusual, step in. If people tend to think of Connecticut as merely a stopover on the way to New England, then this guide exists, in part, to shatter that common misconception. In-the-know travelers know that Connecticut *is* New England, and boasts all its quintessential charms, from romantic escapes and fun family trips to adventurous back-to-nature excursions, without the long drive. Take your pick (or try them all)—and enjoy the trip.

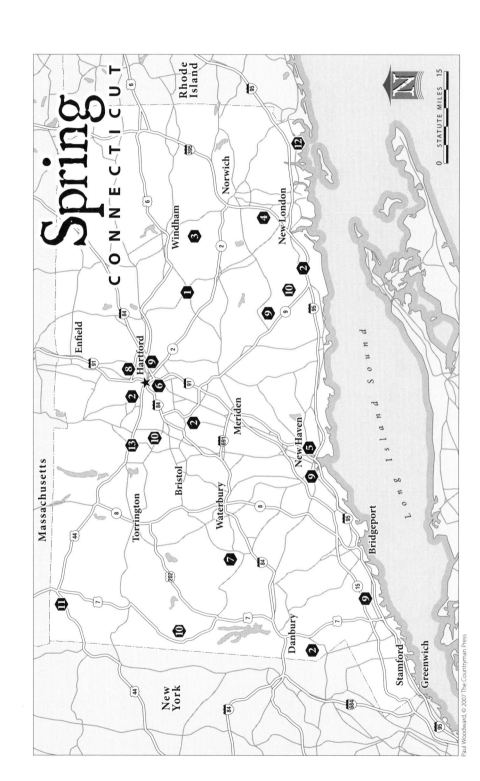

Spring

CONNECTICUT

Massachusetts

Rhode
Island

New
York

Long Island Sound

Enfield
Hartford
Windham
Norwich
New London
Meriden
New Haven
Bristol
Torrington
Waterbury
Danbury
Bridgeport
Stamford
Greenwich

N

0   15
STATUTE MILES

Paul Woodward, © 2007 The Countryman Press

Spring

SWEET DESTINATIONS

Sugarin' Time at Connecticut's Sugarhouses

"Will winter ever end?" That's what many a New Englander is thinking come March. The calendar says spring arrives this month on the 21st, but Mother Nature seems to say differently. Look closely, however, and signs of nature's next act are emerging: In Connecticut, clusters of aluminum buckets hanging from sugar maples along back roads and plumes of wood smoke and fragrant steam curling up into the air are familiar signals that maple syrup season is under way.

I spotted the sign for Wenzel's Sugarhouse on the rural outskirts of Hebron and joined a small crowd in the rustic wooden structure watching Ron Wenzel demo the New England ritual of renewal known as sugaring, so-called for the centuries-old Native American tradition of making maple sugar. The sweet surprise of finding a sugarhouse at work draws winter-weary crowds to the Hebron Maple Festival to watch the art of maple syrup–making unfold and sample nature's sweetest treats, courtesy of *Acer saccharum*.

As winter's chill starts giving way to spring, Wenzel told us, farmers take to the woods with buckets, tubing, drills, and taps; by March, the sap is running and some two hundred family-owned sugarhouses around the state are boiling. Sugaring is usually a solitary operation, but on this day, dressed in blue jeans and heavy-duty work gloves, he patiently answered a

In early spring, sugarhouses around Connecticut are making maple syrup.

flurry of questions, pausing only to stoke and feed the blazing fire that fuels the evaporator and keeps the sap at a steady boil. When an older woman asked what kind of trees he taps, he politely explained that, while all trees have sap, only sugar maple trees produce the sap that's made into maple syrup. Most of us were content to gather quietly around the evaporator, filling our lungs with the sweet steam rising from the lovely amber syrup gurgling and bubbling in wide, shallow pans.

"What's the matter, sap not running in Rhode Island?" Wenzel asked a man surveying the crowd from the open doorway. Their banter shifted to smokestacks and vacuum pumps, hydrometers and evaporators. Fresh sap must be boiled right away, Wenzel and his friend explained, which keeps them working late into the night, sometimes for days at a time.

In late winter, when days are mild but nights remain frosty—syrup makers call it "sugar weather"—it's time for the sap to rise in the trees and start flowing. Sap runs in fits and starts, depending on the weather, which also dictates the length of the sugaring season and the size of the syrup crop. Once nights stay above freezing, leaf buds begin to swell, the sap gets cloudy, and the harvest is over. "Ask me on April first and I'll tell you what kind of season it is," was Wenzel's response to the day's top question. "Until then, it's anyone's guess."

In winters like this one, when a long January thaw tricked the sap into stirring early, he was full-steam ahead in February with 347 taps. While many 21st-century farmers use a maze of plastic tubing, called a pipeline, connecting hundreds of taps to a single holding tank, Wenzel is decidedly old school. He drives a pickup through his stand of sugar maples, emptying pails one by one into a 300-gallon tank. Each day, a 30-year-old tree will yield a gallon of clear, watery sap per tap; of that, 40 gallons boils down to 1 gallon of thick, sweet syrup, which is graded according to color and flavor (grade A for table syrup, grade B for cooking). The cheap stuff in the grocery store, Wenzel noted, is mostly corn sweetener, with less than 5 percent real maple syrup or, in some cases, none at all.

Time-saving innovations aside, it's a labor-intensive job where Mother Nature is boss and profit margins are slim. In 2006, Connecticut farmers put out 61,000 taps and produced 10,000 gallons of syrup, just 1 percent of the 874,000 gallons made in New England (Vermont farmers, by comparison, use 2 million taps annually). By late March, Wenzel has usually boiled down 3,000 gallons of sap into 70 gallons of syrup, a labor of love, to be certain. "If I made one gallon, I'd be happy," he likes to say. "It's a disease with absolutely no cure."

All week I'd been pining for sugar-on-snow, the centuries-old New England treat that pairs hot syrup with fresh snow or shaved ice. But cold rain was falling from a bruised sky when I left the steamy warmth of the sugarhouse, so I settled instead for Joyce Wenzel's warm maple pudding cake, which she topped with homemade maple cream before handing it over.

❋ ❋ ❋ ❋ ❋ ❋ ❋ ❋

IF YOU GO:

The Hebron Maple Festival *(860-649-0841; www.hebron maplefest.com) offers self-guided tours of local sugarhouses, plus family-friendly activities and maple products and treats on the second full weekend in March.* **Getting there:** *From I-84 or I-395 take CT 2 to exit 13, then follow CT 66 east for 6 miles to the center of Hebron.*

❋ ❋ ❋ ❋ ❋ ❋ ❋ ❋

On the way home, I looked past the wet snowflakes hitting the windshield at the sap buckets and fat American robins alongside the road. I've been a New Englander long enough to know that winter always ends like this. But now, to be sure, winter's passing will be sweeter.

MORE MAPLE SUGARING

For a copy of the annual "Guide to Connecticut Sugarhouses" brochure, contact the Connecticut Department of Agriculture (860-713-2569; 1-800-861-9939), 165 Capitol Ave., Hartford, CT 06106. All the sugar-houses listed in the directory are open to the public during the sugaring season, generally late February through mid-April, but it's best to call ahead to get their hours and boiling schedules.

MASTERPIECE WEEKEND

Art Museums

Art lovers take note: Connecticut's art museums run the gamut, from stately repositories for old masters' paintings to showcases for cutting-edge ideas expressed in thoroughly modern works. Together, they are a collection of superlatives. One is the oldest public art museum in the nation. Others include the first devoted to American art, one of the country's original contemporary art museums, and another at the site of a famous American impressionist art colony. Their permanent collections and ever-changing shows offer something to please all manner of aficionado, and they're more welcoming and open than big-city museums, to boot.

Here's a look at some of the stars of Connecticut's art scene:

What the Met is to New York, and the Museum of Fine Arts is to Boston, the **Wadsworth Atheneum Museum of Art** is to Hartford. The country's first public art museum (1842) is still one of the best, not least for its vast cache of some fifty thousand objects that includes Renaissance and French impressionist works, Egyptian artifacts, surrealist paintings, and handcrafted early American furniture. Just as noteworthy: rare 19th-century French sculpture, a collection of costumes and textiles, and Hudson River School masterworks.

"It was what the leading artists in the country were painting at the time the museum was founded," curator Betsy Kornhauser said of the

19th-century art movement led by Thomas Cole and its realistic images of vast wilderness and pastoral idylls painted with reverence and awe. The museum was founded by Daniel Wadsworth, whose colonel father supplied the Continental Army with wool during the Revolution and hosted George Washington whenever the general passed through town.

Spirits were high when I visited the **New Britain Museum of American Art** on a bright April afternoon. One of the state's best-kept secrets was showing its new self to the local media, a dazzling $26 million redo that doubled the museum's size with a dozen new galleries, an auditorium, and a café overlooking historic Walnut Hill Park. A work of art, we agreed, inside and out.

The heart of the museum is, of course, homegrown American art, a collection of five thousand watercolors, oils, sculptures, drawings, and graphics. Curator Maura O'Shea led us through freshly painted downstairs galleries chronicling the history of art from the colonial era to American impressionism, and an open and airy space upstairs, where contemporary works keep house with splendid Thomas Hart Benton murals (the museum's showpiece). While the look is brand new, it is faithful to the original (founded in 1853) in spirit: exclusive devotion to American art.

To be certain, when people talk about cutting-edge art in Connecticut, fashion designer Larry Aldrich's name is usually not far behind, and for good reason: The **Aldrich Contemporary Art Museum**, one of the first such museums in America, was founded in 1964 with his vast private collection.

The Ridgefield gem is alone among the state's museums nurturing and celebrating contemporary art, which is displayed to brilliant effect in a series of small galleries flooded with natural light (some visitors might have to brace themselves for the more provocative exhibits). The museum itself is a stunning work of art, a dramatic combination of tradition (the original 1783 white clapboard building) and modernity (Connecticut granite floors, mahogany ceilings, soaring glass walls). Windows look out on the historic neighborhood and changing exhibits of environmental art in the sculpture garden.

Peter Vanderwarker

New Britain Museum of American Art

It's ironic, perhaps, that the most innovative art space in the state and, some might argue, the country sits snugly in a storybook 18th-century Main Street. But it makes perfect sense: Aldrich, after all, wanted people to experience modern art within their comfort zone.

Florence Griswold didn't intend to host an art colony when she opened her 1817 manse as a summer boardinghouse. But one of her first guests was Henry Ward Ranger, who arrived in 1899 and proclaimed the landscape "only waiting to be painted." "Little did she know, a few years later a boisterous colony of artists would descend upon her house," museum director Jeffrey Anderson said. Today, the **Florence Griswold Museum** includes the national historic landmark home, and fine American art on display in a modern gallery, all set amid lovely natural surroundings.

The impressionist style of painting abstract scenes was all the rage in Europe, and American impressionists loved Connecticut, especially the gentle landscape along the coast. In the next three decades, Childe

❋ ❋ ❋ ❋ ❋ ❋ ❋ ❋

IF YOU GO:

Wadsworth Atheneum Museum of Art *(860-278-2670; www.wadsworthatheneum.org), 600 Main St., Hartford. Open Wednesday through Friday 11–5; Saturday and Sunday 10–5; closed Monday, Tuesday, and major holidays.* **Getting there:** *exit 29A off I-91; exit 48B off I-84 east; exit 54 off I-84 west.*

New Britain Museum of American Art *(860-229-0257; www.nbmaa.org), 56 Lexington St., New Britain. Open Tuesday, Wednesday, and Friday 11–5; Thursday 11–8; Saturday 10–5; Sunday noon–5; closed Monday and major holidays.* **Getting there:** *exit 8 off CT 72 east; exit 7 off CT 72 west; follow signs to the museum.*

Aldrich Museum of Contemporary Art *(203-438-4519; www.aldrichart.org), 258 Main St. (CT 35), Ridgefield. Open Tuesday through Sunday noon–5; closed Monday and major holidays.* **Getting there:** *From I-84 follow US 7 south to the junction of CT 35; the museum is just past the center of Ridgefield.*

Florence Griswold Museum *(860-434-5542; www.florence griswoldmuseum.org), 96 Lyme St., Old Lyme. Open April through December, Tuesday through Saturday 10–5; Sunday 1–5; closed Monday. January through March, Wednesday through Sunday 1–5.* **Getting there:** *exit 70 off I-95; turn left onto CT 156, right onto Halls Road, and left onto Lyme Street.*

❋ ❋ ❋ ❋ ❋ ❋ ❋ ❋

Hassam, William Chadwick, and Willard Metcalf created some of their best works right here in Old Lyme, which became the largest art colony in America devoted to impressionism.

"Florence Griswold was the very soul of the colony," wrote Hassam after he arrived in 1903. The artists' fond tributes to "Miss Florence," as

Old Lyme was an important center for American impressionism when Florence Griswold ran her boardinghouse.

they called her, are the museum's treasures: spontaneous paintings on the door and wall panels—41 in all—a tradition borrowed from European art colonies, particularly those in France (think Giverny) and Holland.

Suffering from *objet* overload? Stroll the historic gardens, tour Chadwick's restored studio, or, better yet, do as 21st-century artists do: Set up an easel and paint *en plein air* the natural beauty that inspired the impressionists.

Miss Florence would surely approve.

HEARTBEAT OF THE REVOLUTION

The Lebanon Green

Until quite recently, everything I knew about the American Revolution I learned from movies, books, and grammar school. What I knew about Lebanon, an agricultural town in northeastern Connecticut, was that it has one of the longest village greens in all New England. I knew its nickname, the "Heartbeat of the American Revolution." And I suspected there was much I didn't know.

Lebanon's role in young America's bid for independence is hardly a secret: Military history buffs, students of early American history, and lovers of New England architecture flock to this bucolic hilltop, where preservation is the byword and an 18th-century winter encampment of French soldiers was a local event tied directly to a major national one. So on a cool and misty May morning, I lit out to find the guardians of history who keep the flame alive and care for Lebanon's proud old buildings.

Who better than Alicia Wayland, Lebanon's town historian, to show me the Jonathan Trumbull Jr. House Museum? I wanted to know the story behind its "Washington slept here" fame. But historians begin at the beginning, so we wandered through the 18th-century Georgian center-chimney farmhouse, admiring the meticulously carved woodwork by Isaac Fitch, Lebanon's master builder, in the keeping room, front parlor, and library. While Trumbull was often overshadowed by his famous father, Wayland said, his achievements were duly notable: comptroller of the U.S. Treasury, member of the first U.S. Congress, and governor of Connecticut for more than a decade. Our last stop was the bedroom where, historians believe, General George Washington stayed on March 4, 1781, on his way to Newport, Rhode Island, to meet with the Comte de Rochambeau. "Washington made Trumbull his military secretary soon after that," Wayland mused. "So he must have made a good impression."

Lebanon tells a familiar New England story—settled by colonists in 1695 on land purchased from local Indians, incorporated in 1700. But one could say it tells the story of colonial America itself, a country in its formative years feeling its first rumblings for independence. And while the first shots of the war were fired at Lexington and Concord, Lebanon is justly proud of its role in the colonies' bid for self-rule, notably, the French-American campaign that led to Washington's victory over the British at Yorktown, Virginia.

Five years into the Revolution, victory was anything but certain for the Continental Army. So Louis XVI sent reinforcements: Some five thousand troops under Rochambeau landed in Rhode Island and marched through Connecticut on the way, ultimately, to rendezvous with Washington's beleaguered men. About 220 cavalry soldiers spent the winter of 1780–81 camped in the fields west of the green, conducting daily drills on the grassy hilltop while Washington and Rochambeau planned war strategy in Wethersfield and Hartford.

I cut across the historic expanse to meet Mary Brown, a member of the Connecticut Daughters of the American Revolution, the group that runs the circa 1740 Governor Jonathan Trumbull (Sr.) House. Connecticut's Revolutionary War governor was arguably one of the nascent United States' most powerful supporters, Brown noted. He was the only colonial governor to defy the crown and one of the Continental Army's key suppliers; his efforts, Washington would later commend, "justly entitled him to the first place among patriots." Nearby in Trumbull's War Office—"Connecticut's Pentagon," as the simple gambrel-roofed building is known—the Council of Safety mobilized the state's war efforts in hundreds of meetings, many stretching late into the night and sometimes including Washington, Lafayette, and Knox. My last stop: the childhood

Governor Jonathan Trumbull's War Office was the headquarters for the Revolutionary War–era Council of Safety.

home of Dr. William Beaumont, known for his pioneering medical research into the physiology of human digestion. Those who love medical macabre will like the bullet extractor, leech jar, Civil War–era battlefield surgical kit, and other 19th-century instruments used to drill, saw, extract, bleed, and stitch.

And then there's the green itself. That iconic rectangle is the heart of many Connecticut towns, and Lebanon's is no exception. Mentally erase the cars and other signs of the 21st century, and it's still 1776 on the mile-long expanse. And it's the genuine article—specifically, one of only a few in New England still in agricultural use.

"It's based on the old tradition from the 1700s," explained Wayland, whose husband is one of the local farmers who cuts hay there. "You're responsible for taking care of the part of the green in front of your home."

I left Wayland, Brown, and others who showed me around to continue what they were doing before my arrival—tidying up their historic buildings for the soon-to-begin season. The 225th anniversary of the Newport-to-Yorktown march, 2006 was a year of major nationwide events marking the campaign, including the unveiling of the Washington-Rochambeau Revolutionary War Route, a 700-mile-long tourist trail tracing the march.

The number of visitors making their way to Lebanon is on the rise, a trend that Sally Whipple, director of the Lebanon Historical Society Museum and Visitor Center, attributes to a growing interest in Connecticut's part in the American colonies' victory over the British.

"Until recently, Massachusetts owned the Revolution," Whipple said. "We didn't have major battles, but we played a critical role."

❊   ❊   ❊   ❊   ❊   ❊   ❊   ❊

IF YOU GO:

Lebanon Historical Society Museum and Visitor Center *(860-642-6579; www.historyoflebanon.org), 856 Trumbull Highway (CT 87), Lebanon. Open year-round, Wednesday through Saturday noon–4 and by appointment. The orientation video is a must-see before touring Lebanon's museums, which are open from mid-May to mid-October. Call each property for its hours of operation, which vary.*

Jonathan Trumbull Jr. House Museum *(860-642-6100; www.jtrumbulljr.org), 780 Trumbull Highway (CT 87).*

Governor Jonathan Trumbull House Museum and Wadsworth Stable *(860-642-7558), 169 West Town St.*

The War Office *(860-873-3399; www.ctssar.org), 149 West Town St.*

Dr. William Beaumont Birthplace *(860-642-6579), 169 West Town St.*

Getting there: *From I-84 east take I-384 (exit 59) to US 6 east; in Andover, take CT 87 to the Lebanon green.*

❊   ❊   ❊   ❊   ❊   ❊   ❊   ❊

Casino Culture

Mohegan Sun and Foxwoods Resort Casino

Wish you were rich? Of course you do. So do I. Who doesn't pine for millions to throw around? Why else would Americans spend $25 billion each year on lottery tickets? For many, the trip to southeastern Connecticut is a journey of hope. No doubt about it: The face of gambling (a pastime I've never fully understood), not to mention the rural landscape along the Thames River, was altered forever in the 1990s when the Mashantucket Pequot and Mohegan tribes received federal recognition. In quick succession, Foxwoods Resort Casino and Mohegan Sun morphed into flourishing gambling empires, a powerhouse combination that brings in 25 million visitors and $2.2 billion a year and gives Atlantic City and Vegas a run for their money.

Suddenly, Connecticut had a serious gaming scene, with the largest casinos in the world a day's drive from the East Coast's biggest cities. If you go to gamble, you're set 24/7; if you're like me, there's plenty for you, too: nonstop nightlife, for starters, not to mention top-flight entertainment, celebrity chefs, and fancy shopping. So take your pick, east side of the Thames River or west, and let the games begin.

WEST OF THE RIVER: MOHEGAN SUN, UNCASVILLE

Gambler or not, from the moment you set foot inside Mohegan Sun, you fall under its spell. It's an architectural stunner, fresh off a billion-dollar expansion. The result? More than 60 restaurants and boutiques, a 1,200-room luxury hotel and spa, 6,000-plus slot machines, and perhaps most important, big-bucks decor with an eye on the past.

"When we first received federal recognition, the Mohegan tribe only had one building, the Mohegan church, which was designed by missionaries and not our choice of architecture," explained Melissa Tantaquidgeon-Zobel, who heads the Mohegan's cultural and community programs, and whose great-aunt is Gladys Tantaquidgeon, the tribe's 104-year-old medicine woman. "It occurred to the tribe that if we got funding to make an architectural statement, we wanted it to literally shout that it was Mohegan."

And so it does. Colors, designs, and building materials are drawn from Mohegan art and tradition, with stories worked in as well. Water cascades seven stories down Taughannick Falls; nearby, a Dale

Playing the slots at Mohegan Sun: Connecticut's casinos attract millions of visitors.

Chihuly–designed 10,000-pound handblown glass sculpture soars above the casino floor. Wombi Rock, a magnificent three-story creation of onyx quarried from Iran, Pakistan, and Mexico, doubles as a multilevel lounge. The hotel's multifaceted glass exterior resembles the quartz crystal used in trade and ceremonial objects; a fragrant cedar "forest" with waterfalls and reflecting pools fills the lobby.

Later, we dressed up for a dinner at Tuscany, celebrity chef Todd English's place, then strolled the Casino of the Earth and watched the endless and always-amusing parade passing by on the casino floor, where live music spilling out of the Wolf Den mingled with the kind of frenetic clanging that comes from thousands of slot machines. From a cozy banquette in the Cabaret Theater, we listened to Frank Sinatra Jr. croon his father's hits to a delighted crowd, then sipped martinis at Lucky's Lounge, a Vegas-inspired hot spot.

In the end, we hit the eat, drink, and be merry trifecta, and we didn't even gamble. There was too much else to do. That brief getaway also brought a revelation: The 21st-century American casino experience is a brand-new game. Here, I reflected, is a place as laid-back or glitzy as one chose to make it. As a weekend getaway, it has something for all of us. You can bet on it.

EAST OF THE RIVER: FOXWOODS RESORT CASINO, MASHANTUCKET

The spectacle of Foxwoods rising majestically out of southeastern Connecticut's green rolling hills has been described in many ways, but it's most definitely spectacular, if not a glittering over-the-rainbow fantasyland. If you come to the largest casino on the planet for the gaming, of course you'll be in luck (if not lucky). If not, there are many diversions from championship golf at the Lake-of-Isles resort to top-rate blues at Club BB King. In every direction, throngs of tour bus gamblers and superhigh rollers buzzing around the place give plenty to watch—that is, if you can break away from one of the 7,400 slot machines.

Foxwoods is a collection of superlatives: The first casino in Connecticut, the world's biggest bingo hall, the largest Native American museum. To be

Foxwoods Resort Casino offers a free shuttle to the Mashantucket Pequot Museum and Research Center.

sure, there is gambling galore—slots, blackjack, poker, roulette—and for some visitors, this is reason enough. For everyone else, the latest $700 million hotel and casino expansion emphasizes what, in casinospeak, is called "nongaming" entertainment. Like the only Hard Rock Cafe between Boston and New York, whose walls are lined with rock 'n' roll memorabilia (think Steven Tyler guitar and Isaac Hayes cape). For upscale dining, high rollers head high above Foxwoods and don't blink at the $40-something entrées at Paragon. It's on a short list of Connecticut restaurants to earn the prestigious AAA Four Diamond award.

And while there are many reasons to visit a big, glitzy casino, touring a museum is rarely one of them. Here is an exception. We hopped the free shuttle to the Mashantucket Pequot Museum and Research Center, a hidden treasure among Connecticut's trove of museums. The centerpiece of this top-notch facility devoted to Native American history is a collection of remarkably lifelike dioramas, with subjects ranging from the Pequot War to a 16th-century Native American village. We promised to return in August for the Pequot tribe's annual Schemitzun Powwow, a "feast of green corn and dance" that draws participants from hundreds of tribes across the country; its authentic traditions and artistry are reminders of where this casino culture all began.

Hard to beat that hand.

※ ※ ※ ※ ※ ※ ※ ※

IF YOU GO:

Mohegan Sun *(1-888-226-7711; www.mohegansun.com), One Mohegan Sun Blvd., Uncasville.* **Getting there:** *exit 79A off I-395.*

Foxwoods Resort Casino *(1-800-369-9663; www.foxwoods.com), 39 Norwich-Westerly Rd. (CT 2), Mashantucket. The* **Mashantucket Pequot Museum & Research Center** *(1-800-411-9671; www.pequot museum.org), 110 Pequot Trail, Mashantucket, is open daily 9–5; closed major holidays.* **Getting there:** *exit 92 (CT 2 west) off I-95; from Hartford take I-84 east to exit 55 (CT 2 east).*

※ ※ ※ ※ ※ ※ ※ ※

Intelligent Design

Yale University

I hate feeling clueless, especially when I'm surrounded by the kind of extremely intelligent people like those at one of the world's top institutions of higher learning. In this case, I'm on the storied campus of Yale University, where for intellectual stimulation or artistic inspiration, visitors need look no further than the museums, theaters, galleries, and full roster of events—many of them free of charge—that are open to all but are often overlooked or, simply, unknown.

For not a few people, Yale is where New Haven's heart beats loudest. To be sure, the Elm City has a cosmopolitan vibe all its own, but the influence of the Ivy League community lends a worldly tone to the historic city that gave the United States the cotton gin, Frisbee, the municipal public library, and clam pizza. In the finest college-town tradition, a vibrant scene bustles around campus, mostly along Chapel Street, where visiting scholars and other literati are apt to be found perusing the stacks at Atticus, whose café provides caffeinated inspiration to weary students.

The uninitiated, like me, need some help pulling it together. So when I found myself in New Haven one blustery February afternoon, I joined one of the daily campus tours. Our guide, an amicable sophomore named Leland, promised we would walk, literally, through Yale's 300-plus-year-old tradition of educating some of history's biggest players—Nathan Hale,

A guide holds forth on the Yale campus tour.

Noah Webster, every U.S. president since 1989—and get a front-seat look at what makes Yale so, well, Yale.

On the edge of the city's 1638 green, we left the 21st century behind and passed through Phelps Gate onto Old Campus, where Connecticut Hall, New Haven's oldest building (1750), housed students like Hale and (not simultaneously) William Howard Taft. Yale is famed for its imposing Gothic-style buildings, but campus architecture runs a surprising gamut, from classic collegiate Gothic (Harkness Tower) to sublime (Beinecke Rare Book and Manuscript Library), provocative (Yale Center for British Art) to awe inspiring (Woolsey Hall).

Leland's spiel was flawless, but we loved the behind-the-scenes glimpses best: The cloistered world of Branford College, one of a dozen residential colleges (modeled after Oxford, Cambridge, and Harvard) whose courtyard Robert Frost called one of the prettiest places he'd ever seen. The cathedral-like Sterling Memorial Library, where students hunched over books in dim alcoves. The tales behind the extrawide door in Connecticut Hall, the Y-shaped cracks in dorm windows, even a covert CIA mission involving a statue of the patriot Hale (Yale 1773).

In the end, it was the Yalies themselves, hustling past our wide-eyed group, that fascinated us most of all. Stressed by midterms? Fantasizing about spring break? Annoyed by our stares? Maybe just the kind of studied seriousness it takes to get into one of the world's top universities.

But we couldn't help ourselves. After all, who knows which might become the next George W. Bush or Bill Clinton, which might blossom into the next Meryl Streep or Paul Newman, which could be another Nathan Hale?

MORE YALE

A campus tour is an obvious attraction, but as Yale is the only Ivy League university with a professional arts school, concertgoers and theater lovers have plenty of options, namely, hundreds of performances (many of them free) staged throughout the year. If you feel Yale's artistic community might be snooty or stodgy, it's simply not so. Case in point: Before a Woolsey Hall concert, a music professor shared this from-the-heart observation: "He's a really nice guy." *He* being Sir Neville Marriner, under whose baton Yale's Camerata, Schola Cantorum, Glee Club, and Philharmonia breathed new life into works spanning Mozart's career. The 1771 *Regina Coeli* was a treat. The *Coronation Mass* was another bright spot, and a stir-

❋ ❋ ❋ ❋ ❋ ❋ ❋ ❋

IF YOU GO:

Yale University *(general information: 203-432-3200; sports hotline: 203-432-9253; www.yale.edu), New Haven. Guided tours leave from the visitors information center at 149 Elm St. Monday through Friday at 10:30 and 2, Saturday and Sunday at 1:30. No tours on the day of the Yale-Harvard football game or during winter break.* **Getting there:** *From I-95 pick up I-91 north and take exit 3 (Trumbull Street); turn left onto Prospect Street, then left onto Elm Street to reach the visitors center.*

Yale School of Music *(203-432-4158);* **Yale Repertory Theatre** *(203-432-1234), 112 Chapel St.;* **Yale Cabaret** *(203-432-1566), 217 Park St.;* **Yale Center for British Art** *(203-432-2800), 1080 Chapel St.;* **Yale University Art Gallery** *(203-432-0600), 1111 Chapel St.;* **Beinecke Rare Book & Manuscript Library** *(203-432-2972), 121 Wall St.;* **Yale Collection of Musical Instruments** *(203-432-0822), 15 Hillhouse Ave.*

See also **Peabody Museum of National History** *(chapter 46)*

❋ ❋ ❋ ❋ ❋ ❋ ❋ ❋

ring version of the *Solemn Vespers* concluded the tribute to the composer whose genius—and 250th birthday—the world was feting this year.

Paul Mellon (Yale 1929) had a passion for British art, and the means to amass quite a bit of it, which now resides at the Yale Center for British Art, a brazenly modern Louis Kahn–designed masterpiece. It's the most extensive collection of works—outside the United Kingdom—reflecting British life, art, and culture since medieval times: thousands of paintings, sculptures, drawings, watercolors, and prints, as well as rare manuscripts and books. No less impressive is another Kahn gem—the newly made-over Yale University Art Gallery, the country's oldest college art museum (1832), founded with the gift by John Trumbull of his paintings of the American Revolution. Among the highlights: American art, early 20th-century European works, and Roman artifacts—in all, more than 185,000 treasures from ancient times to the present.

Across campus, the Beinecke Rare Book & Manuscript Library is a quiet gem among Yale's well-known treasures. The collection of 750,000 books and several million manuscripts includes originals by Mark Twain and Charles Dickens, not to mention medieval texts, ancient papyrus documents, and a 1455 Gutenberg Bible, the world's first printed book. The windowless building is an architectural marvel: one hundred panels of thin, translucent marble cast a surreal glow and protect the rarities inside from the sun's infrared and ultraviolet rays. Another jewel is the Yale University Collection of Musical Instruments, started in 1900 by the piano manufacturer Steinert and today boasting a cache of rarities and a concert series featuring many of the collection's antique instruments. The aspiring actors gracing the stages of the Yale School of Drama, the Yale Repertory Theatre, and the Yale Cabaret have some impressive predecessors—besides Streep and Newman they include Sigourney Weaver, Jodie Foster, John Turturro, and Frances McDormand.

Yale has a long tradition of athletics, which began with rowing in 1843 and manifests itself in the annual football game against Ivy rival Harvard, played on the Saturday before Thanksgiving. Harvard-Yale is the biggest party night of the year: The Bulldogs have been tangling with the Crimson on the gridiron since 1875, and the annual contest offers collegiate football and tailgating in the finest sense. In 1889, Yale became the first university in America to adopt a mascot, a bulldog named Handsome Dan. Today, you might spot Handsome Dan XVI on the sidelines.

What could be more Yale than that?

ALL THE PRETTY HORSES
The New England Carousel Museum and the Bushell Park Carousel

What does a dollar buy? In Hartford's Bushnell Park, it's good for one nostalgic trip via 1914 merry-go-round, where a marvelously sculpted stallion will take you on a headlong gallop straight back to your childhood while a Wurlitzer band organ grinds out old-time tunes.

In the shadow of skyscrapers and the State Capitol, the carousel that came to Connecticut's capital city from an Ohio amusement park in 1974 has a new lease on life. The yellow pine platform, once hidden beneath years of paint and polish, gleams like new. Machinery has been spiffed up with newly applied 23-carat gold leaf, and the 24-sided pavilion sparkles and shines with stained glass, mirrored panels, and eight hundred twinkling white lights.

Of the 6,000 carousels built between 1880 and 1930, fewer than two hundred remain; of those, Bushnell Park's is one of only three hand-sculpted by Solomon Stein and Harry Goldstein, the renowned Russian master carvers who, like many immigrant artisans, came to the United States at the dawn of the carousel craze. Their trademark over-the-top flamboyance, the style known as Coney Island, meant big, powerful animals with nostrils flaring and tongues lolling, sporting gold buckles and carved cabbage roses, jewel-encrusted saddles and bridles.

Hartford's treasure has felt the ravages of time, not to mention the

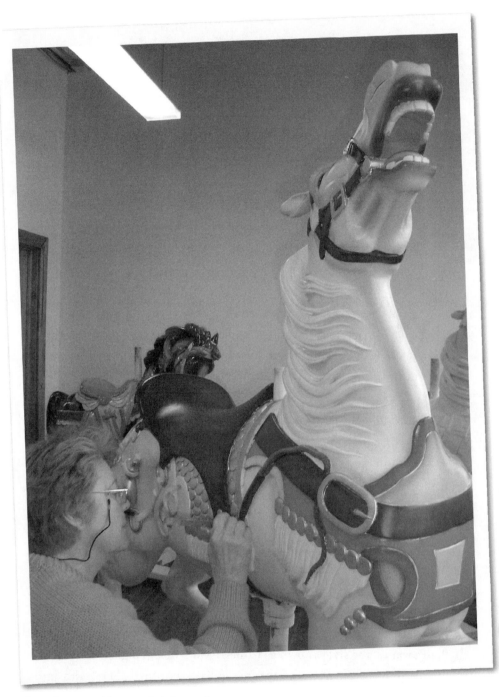

Returning carousel horses to their former glory

100,000 children (and children at heart) who ride it every year. So in 2006, one by one the horses traveled 18 miles away to Bristol, to a restoration shop above the New England Carousel Museum, where 21st-century artisans transformed the faded antiques into beautiful examples of American folk art.

It was the carousel's first major overhaul in two decades, and a massive undertaking: The herd suffered from a host of maladies, from wood rot and missing tails to broken legs and crackling paint. Jumpers, prancers, and standers—48 horses in all—and two "lovers' chariots" passed through the shop for a top-to-bottom makeover entailing about 40 hours of sanding and woodwork and another 40 hours of painting per steed.

On a snowy Wednesday afternoon in early March, I watched in silence as Judy Baker's steady hand expertly blurred the line between reality and fantasy as she worked on one of the mares. She's a second-row horse, the master painter told me without lifting her eyes from her work, and lovely: creamy white coat, bared teeth, and wild, flowing mane. The museum's master carver had already stripped, sanded, and primed her so that Baker could apply turn-of-the-century oils to the bridle, saddle, buckles, blanket, mane, and shoes in painstaking detail.

Each brushstroke pulled me a bit farther back in time, to the 1970s, to be exact. It was a time when just about every kid I knew rode merry-go-rounds. In Connecticut, that likely meant the Bushnell Park carousel. It all came rushing back: the mad dash across the wooden platform to reach that perfect horse before anyone else did. They were all so beautiful—the milky white mare wearing a jewel-encrusted bridle, the ebony stallion with bulging eyes and golden saddle. The best, of course, were the jumpers that moved up and down in time to the blaring music. Second choice, a prancer whose front hooves pawed the air as if trying to free itself, it always seemed to me, from the pole tethering it to the platform.

The museum, which manages the city-owned carousel, also boasts one of the most extensive collections of antique carousel horses in the 1country. "Just as you would walk into an art museum and spot a Van Gogh or a Monet, you could walk onto a carousel and see different styles of carving," explained Louise DeMars, the museum's director, as she walked me through the main gallery and instructed me on what to look for. County fair–style horses are diminutive and plain figures with no protruding pieces that could break off in transit from one fair to another. The gold-and-glitz Coney Island horses are all gold and glitz. Philadelphia-style horses, in comparison, are amazingly lifelike. "We always joke that if you put an apple in front of his nose, he would probably eat it," DeMars said of one of the museum's prized pieces.

What began as military training for 17th-century knights and noblemen eventually evolved into a rite of passage for many 20th-century youngsters, and a nod to the era when people went to amusement parks dressed in their Sunday best and the carousel was a park's centerpiece, not just one of the kiddie rides.

"Our mission isn't just to restore antique carousel horses; we're educating the next generation of carousel lovers," DeMars said of the children

IF YOU GO:

New England Carousel Museum *(860-585-5411; www.the carouselmuseum.com), 95 Riverside Ave. (CT 72), Bristol. Open April through November, Monday through Saturday 10–5, Sunday noon–5; December through March, Thursday through Saturday 10–5, Sunday noon–5; closed major holidays.* **Getting there:** *From I-84 east take exit 31 (exit 33 off I-84 west) to Bristol, follow CT 72 west to the museum.*

Bushnell Park Carousel *(860-585-5411), Bushnell Park, Jewell and Elm Streets (next to the State Capitol), Hartford. The carousel operates from May to mid-October, Thursday through Sunday 11–5; closed on Monday and rainy days.* **Getting there:** *From I-84 west take exit 48A (exit 48 off I-84 east). At the end of the exit ramp, turn right onto Asylum Street, following the edge of the park. The carousel is on the left, past the Memorial Arch.*

CORY MAZON

A favorite childhood pastime

that pass through the museum. "I make them promise to come back and bring their kids and grandkids to ride.

When I took a ride to Bushnell Park a few months later, I knew the horse I wanted. This time I wasn't seeking out a particular color or stance. When I spotted the pink and red saddle blanket, I hopped on and ran my finger along the reins made new by Judy Baker's expert hand. We were young and old, whisked around on wooden ponies prancing up and down in time to the Wurlitzer's nostalgic melody. Some of us were reliving sweet childhood memories, while for others, memories were in the making.

Less than four minutes had passed, yet I felt like I'd traveled far.

Antiques Heaven
Woodbury

Those looking for antiques shops will hit the mother lode in Woodbury, where a love affair with the past makes the local trade a hot destination for serious collectors searching for rare and important pieces, home decorators on the lookout for the latest thing, and others just learning how to collect and enjoy old things.

With some 50 dealers in town, mostly in centuries-old dwellings up and down Main Street, it's not only the "Antiques Capital of Connecticut," but also one of New England's top spots for the buying and selling of vintage wares. Shop owners scour the globe for sought-after antiquities from the 16th through 20th centuries: rare finds from Europe and Asia, treasures from the Federal period and the Victorian era, antique jewelry that would give today's bling a run for its money, and relics of young America's earliest days, the objects our ancestors used to adorn their drawing rooms, libraries, and bedchambers.

While I'm no collector, I decided to take the winding back road route to this bustling hub of things past one warm spring morning and have a chat with some of these specialists in antiques.

What shops are the best depends, of course, on what you're looking for. A good place to begin, I'm told, is Eleish-van Breems Antiques and its stock of 18th- and 19th-century Scandinavian furniture. In their inviting

Woodbury is known as the Antiques Capital of Connecticut.

shop, Rhonda Eleish and Edie van Breems have assembled a mixture of antique furniture (think painted cupboards and armoires) and home accessories (vintage copper kitchenware). If you've come to splurge, a late 18th-century Swedish cupboard will set you back $10,000, but for those on a tighter budget, there are reproductions, some collectibles in their own right. When I dropped by, bold and bright Marimekko linens were among the candles, bath salts, and other items that make chic and inexpensive gifts; I made a mental note to return come holiday-shopping time.

It's just a short hop down the road to Country Loft Antiques, where French antiques are something of a specialty. Carole Weiner's emporium on a lovely 19-acre estate is one of the oldest in town, where accoutrements from French vineyards fill a silo–turned–wine cellar. Continue your foray at the Elemental Garden, a one-stop treasure trove of English and French garden antiques as well as an extraordinary assortment of vintage gardening tools and gas lanterns. Have your heart set on a 19th-century carved stone urn? Resisting the temptation to snap it up, I settled for browsing instead.

Suddenly I understood why so many out-of-towners spend the weekend here: You could spend many hours wandering from the French Canadian painted cupboards at Monique Shay Antiques to the old-master paintings at Jennings and Rohn Antiques, the horse-drawn buggies and sleighs at Antiques on Main, and the Mill House's 18th- and 19th-century English and French furniture. At the heart of town, there's Madeline West Antiques, with paintings and antique porcelains, and the Stone & Picket, filled with historically accurate colonial reproduction lighting. A few doors away, Wayne Pratt, Inc. specializes in fine American antiques and primitive portraits.

From there, you can amble over to Wayne Mattox Antiques. With more than two decades in the business, Mattox is no stranger to antiquity. Filling his gracious 19th-century Greek-revival house is an ever-changing roster that on my visit included a document signed by Abraham Lincoln, a 19th-century weathervane, a signed Picasso print, and an early 19th-century English mahogany desk that caught my eye. As it was a little beyond my price range ($15,000), I opted instead to quiz Mattox about antiques and the people who love them.

"Long ago as a society we deemed old beautiful objects as a sign of our wealth and production," he said. "And like real estate, there's only a certain amount of them."

It used to be that the older and rarer a piece, the better. "Now an antique is anything that made a difference in its day, either artistically or from a technological or marketing standpoint," he explained, pointing to Coca-Cola advertising as an example. "It opened the door to millions of objects produced in the 20th century."

My last stop was Grass Roots Antiques, run by Ethel Greenblatt, one of the first dealers to come to town in the 1970s. Her shop in a former silk mill is packed with a something-for-everyone mix of objects, from sparkling chandeliers and Limoges china to glass cases full of what antiques collectors refer to as "smalls," meaning items that fit in your hand.

"Woodbury is, well, antique-y," she said, when asked about its appeal. "There are no malls, no busy Main Street. It's the kind of town that lends itself to antiques."

Mattox describes Woodbury as "antiques-fertile." "We're surrounded by things that would otherwise be found in museums," he said. "Where else can you drive around at night and see highboys in the windows? Pieces have been in some of these homes for more than two hundred years."

I didn't find anything to buy, and that's fine, because mostly I'd come to Woodbury to look. I picked my way through paintings and Persian rugs, statuary and silverware, and finally decided I needed nothing.

But if I did, I knew where to find it.

❊ ❊ ❊ ❊ ❊ ❊ ❊ ❊

IF YOU GO:

The Woodbury Antiques Dealers Association *(www.antiques woodbury.com) publishes an online guide to the shops in town. At the* **Woodbury Antiques & Flea Market** *(www.woodburyfleamarket.com), 787 Main St. South, thrifty shoppers go trawling among 120 vendors for trinkets, treasures, and tchotchkes on Saturday mornings mid-March through December.* **Getting there:** *From 1-84 east take exit 15 and follow US 6 to Woodbury; from 1-84 west take exit 17 and follow CT 64 west to Woodbury.*

❊ ❊ ❊ ❊ ❊ ❊ ❊ ❊

NEW ENGLAND'S RISING STAR

Hartford

"**O**f all the beautiful towns it has been my fortune to see this is the chief," Mark Twain once raved. "You do not know what beauty is if you have not been here." A keen 19th-century traveler, Twain was referring not to London, Paris, or Rome, but to Hartford.

It's been some time since Connecticut's capital garnered such accolades—Hartford has long been characterized as a place where sidewalks roll up at 5 PM—but a renaissance is under way that's bringing plenty of attention to this low-profile city settled by Massachusetts Puritans in 1636. Historic old buildings are sprucing themselves up as new ones rise along the Connecticut River, thanks in large part to an ambitious $775 million downtown redevelopment project called Adriaen's Landing that includes riverfront parks, a state-of-the-art science center, upscale condos, and a new convention center.

Hartford, which now bills itself as "New England's Rising Star," is polishing its image and emerging new as a vibrant capital where people not only work, but live. For visitors, trendy restaurants, museums and theater, a vibrant arts scene, and an eclectic mix of attractions are but a few of the surprises waiting in this city on the rise.

ARTS SPACES

It was a chilly night in Hartford, yet a warm glow emanated from the

Hartford's Capitol is known for its iconic gold dome.

former Underwood Typewriter factory in the city's Parkville neighborhood. Inside it hummed with energy as arts lovers mingled over martinis and checked out brand-new art installations while a lively Brazilian quintet heated up the night even more.

The popular monthly art and cocktail soiree drew about four hundred people to one of Connecticut's unique art spaces and one of Hartford's best-kept secrets. Real Art Ways—or RAW, as it's known—opened in 1975 as an alternative venue for artists and musicians.

"There's a feeling you'd expect from a much more sophisticated city than Hartford," said Will Wilkins, RAW's longtime director. Events range from live music (jazz, classical, hip-hop, techno) and art exhibitions to indie films, literary readings, even a family film festival.

While the words "edgy" and "eclectic" leap to mind when describing this art gallery-cum-independent-cinema-cum-performance space, the casual, friendly vibe is refreshingly unpretentious. "We provide a warm and welcoming environment where everyone can feel comfortable," Wilkins said, then added, "It's within everyone's capacity to enjoy contemporary art."

Later, we headed across town to the Bushnell Center for the Performing Arts, where the Hartford Symphony, under the baton of music director Edward Cumming, was performing Beethoven's masterpiece Ninth Symphony for a packed house. It was the "concert of the season," the program read, and the composer's "Ode to Joy" was made even more poignant by nearly two hundred voices from Connecticut's top choral groups. A recent $45 million expansion had given Hartford's premier arts venue world-class status, and many visitors milling around the lobby were seeing its new look for the first time. Also here: Broadway touring shows, dance performances, music, and stand-up comedy.

NOW AND THEN

If marble, stained glass, and gilt could talk! Save for Governor M. Jodi Rell's press conference, Connecticut's gold-domed Capitol was eerily quiet. Jim, our crimson-jacketed tour guide, explained the absence of lawyers and lobbyists: The legislature wasn't in session.

Hartford's Wolf Pack plays home games at the Civic Center.

"It's like a church in here," the lady from Indianapolis whispered in the rotunda, 257 feet below the building's iconic gold dome. Indeed, when the Gothic-revival masterpiece of soaring arches, sweeping staircases, and hushed alcoves was completed in 1878, the day's top architects lauded its design (Frank Lloyd Wright, however, called it "ridiculous").

In the plush Senate chamber, we each took a turn in the lieutenant governor's seat, the so-called "wishing chair." "Legend says that whoever sits here wishes to be governor," Jim said as I rubbed the ornately carved armrests and scanned the magnificent room where lawmakers would soon tackle high energy costs and gridlock on I-95. "Not me," I said with absolute certainty.

Afterward, I walked over to the Old State House, built of Connecticut brick and brownstone in 1796. Exhibits tell the story of the first settlers, who fled the rigid rules of the Massachusetts colony, and of Hartford founder Thomas Hooker, whose fiery sermon sparked the Fundamental Orders of 1638–39, which historians believe was the world's first written constitution (hence Connecticut's "Constitution State" nickname). The gloriously refurbished legislative chambers and Supreme Court room stand in stark contrast to the offbeat Museum of Oddities and Curiosities, but both are worth a visit.

* * * * * * * *

IF YOU GO:

Real Art Ways *(860-232-1006; www.realartways.org), 56 Arbor St. Gallery and cinema open Tuesday through Sunday; closed Monday.*

Bushnell Center for the Performing Arts *(860-987-5900, 1-888-824-2874; www.bushnell.org) and* **Hartford Symphony** *(860-244-2999; www.hartfordsymphony.org), 166 Capitol Ave.*

Old State House *(860-522-6766; www.ctosh.org), 800 Main St. Open Tuesday through Friday 11–5; Saturday 10–5; closed Sunday and Monday.*

Connecticut State Capitol *(860-240-0222; www.cga.ct.gov/ capitoltours), 210 Capitol Ave. Free guided tours of the Capitol and legislative office building, September through June, Monday through Friday; Saturday tours of the Capitol building from April through October.*

Bushnell Park *(860-232-6710; www.bushnellpark.org), downtown*

Elizabeth Park *(860-231-9443; www.elizabethpark.org), at the corner of Prospect and Asylum Avenues.*

Hartford Wolf Pack *(860-548-2000; www.hartfordwolfpack.com) plays home games at the Hartford Civic Center from October to mid-April.*

Connecticut Science Center *(860-727-0457; www.ctscience center.org), 50 Columbus Blvd.*

Getting there: *A dozen or so exits off I-91 north- and southbound and I-84 east- and westbound lead downtown. Amtrak (1-800-872-7245; www.amtrak.com) and major bus lines operate from Union Station.*

See also Hartford Stage (chapter 9), Wadsworth Atheneum Museum of Art (chapter 2), Bushnell Park Carousel (chapter 6).

* * * * * * * *

TAKE IT OUTSIDE

The concept of city parks dates to the Victorian age, when grassy expanses with shade trees and walking paths provided a quiet retreat in overcrowded cities. Hartford's Bushnell Park was America's first, predating even Manhattan's Central Park. The historic landscape is the heart of the city, "the front lawn of the Capitol," said Susan Wallace of the Bushnell Park Foundation. For visitors, there's a vintage carousel (see chapter 6), concerts, guided walks, and tours of the Gothic brownstone 19th-century Soldiers and Sailors Memorial Arch.

In June, rose enthusiasts head to Elizabeth Park, America's first public rose garden, where the specialties of the house—roses, and lots of them—are in peak splendor. It's also the country's first All-America Test Garden, where rosarians (rose experts, in case you didn't know) evaluate new varieties of the thorny beauties for fragrance, foliage, and other characteristics.

In June, rose lovers head for Hartford's Elizabeth Park.

Rose season aside, there are gardens galore, plus a café and a full schedule of concerts, lectures, and tours.

Bring the Family

If you were a Whalers fan in the 1980s—and who wasn't?—then you remember the void left when the city's beloved NHL team left town. Today, the minor-league Hartford Wolf Pack has a rabid following in two camps: those who miss the Whalers, and those who just love hockey.

"If people were hockey fans in Hartford before the Wolf Pack got here, then we know we're connecting with some of them," says director of broadcasting Bob Crawford, who also does the team's play-by-play. "But many of the kids in the stands never saw the Whalers play. They're here to see the Wolf Pack."

As this book goes to press, the new Connecticut Science Center's dramatic glass towers are rising above the Connecticut River. The $150 million state-of-the-art interactive science museum is slated for a 2008 opening, with hands-on exhibits and family programs.

A Storied History

Theater in Connecticut

I could have sat in my comfy ruby-red upholstered chair all night. Lured by the buzz surrounding the $17.8 million renovation that closed **Westport Country Playhouse** for the first time since World War II, I ventured down to the tony Fairfield County suburbs for a look see, and to catch the opening night presentation of the comedy *On the Verge.* I glanced around the refurbished, restored, and reglorified playhouse—the new seats and orchestra pit, improved sightlines, and, perhaps most important, heating and air conditioning, that enables the longtime summer theater to stay open year-round. Despite its dramatic makeover and star-studded lineups, I noted with relief, it has held on to the intimate and informal qualities of its beginnings, from the rustic timbers to the signature red drapes, and, on display, handbills and programs from the early days.

The iconic red barn has been attracting crowds with notable casts and a lineup of revivals, new treats, and old standbys since 1931, when Broadway producers Lawrence Langner and Armina Marshall turned what was a 19th-century tannery into a summer place to try out new works away from Broadway. Stories are told of the stars who graced the stage: Westporter Paul Newman (whose wife Joanne Woodward was, until recently, the theater's longtime artistic director), Ethel Barrymore, Liza Minnelli, Gene Wilder, Henry Fonda. Even the roster of past interns reads like a who's who of stage and screen: Larry Hagman, Stephen

Sondheim, Cary Elwes, Tammy Grimes.

While the hilarious Victorian-era tale of time-traveling sisters was pure pleasure, the night's big moment came before the show, when artistic director Tazewell Thompson hinted at big news: Legendary actor James Earl Jones would star in *Thurgood*, a one-man play about Supreme Court Justice Thurgood Marshall that would premiere at the playhouse before taking a shot at Broadway.

The Learned Ladies of Park Avenue *at Hartford Stage*

T. CHARLES ERICKSON

Hartford audiences are a lucky bunch. Musicals, plays, classics, provocative new works . . . the folks at **Hartford Stage** have got them covered. Connecticut's oldest regional theater—established in 1964—is a Tony Award winner (the trophy is proudly on display in the lobby).

I visited on a quiet January morning with Paul Marte, the theater's public relations manager. A full season of shows was under way, the stage set for New London–native Eugene O'Neill's *A Moon for the Misbegotten*, the Nobel Prize–winning final work by America's greatest playwright. Performances take place in a small theater with 489 seats surrounding the stage. "'Intimate' is a word we hear people use often when describing the space," Marte said. "There's an up-close view from anywhere in the house."

The theater draws its audience locally, so much so, in fact, that it successfully shares productions with New Haven's venerable Long Wharf Theatre, just 40 miles away. "It's unusual for two theaters so close to one another," Marte acknowledged. "But in Connecticut, somehow, it works."

❋ ❋ ❋ ❋ ❋ ❋ ❋ ❋

IF YOU GO:

Westport Country Playhouse *(203-227-4177; www.westport playhouse.org), 25 Powers Court (off US 1), Westport.* **Getting there:** *exit 17 off I-95 north; exit 18 off I-95 south.*

Hartford Stage *(860-525-5601; www.hartfordstage.org), 50 Church St., Hartford.* **Getting there:** *exit 32B off I-91; exit 50 off I-84 west or exit 49 off I-84 east.*

Shubert Theater *(203-562-5666, 1-888-736-2663; www.shubert.com), 247 College St., New Haven.* **Getting there:** *exit 47 off I-95; exit 1 off I-91; exit 57 off the Merritt Parkway, and follow CT 34 to downtown.*

Goodspeed Opera House *(860-873-8668; www.goodspeed.org), Goodspeed Landing, CT 82, East Haddam.* **Getting there:** *exit 7 off CT 9; turn left at the end of the ramp, then turn right at the traffic light.*

❋ ❋ ❋ ❋ ❋ ❋ ❋ ❋

It's a real show-biz story: On the floor of New Haven's **Shubert Theater**, an unknown actress (Barbara Cook) spied a slip of paper, sheet music to an unfamiliar show (*The King and I*) by two fledgling composers (Rodgers and Hammerstein). Cook, who played the historic theater in the 1940s, held on to it. "She knew that if it was going to be at the Shubert, it was eventually going to become something big," public relations director Anthony Lupinacci said.

The before-they-were-famous tale should come as no surprise to anyone familiar with the Shubert's reputation of nurturing stars on their way to the top. What really puts the theater on the map, however, is its history—at a time when Broadway was the artistic heart of American culture, more Broadway shows were born on the Shubert's stage than at any other theater in the world. "Its history is what solidified its future," Lupinacci said. "There isn't even a theater on Broadway that can boast the number of national and world premieres that have happened here."

Since 1914, the "Birthplace of the Nation's Greatest Hits" has seen 'em all, from *The Sound of Music* and *The King and I* to *My Fair Lady*. During my visit, stage and film icon Lynn Redgrave was playing the estimable Lady Bracknell in *The Importance of Being Earnest*, a new production of Oscar Wilde's masterpiece about mistaken identity in 19th-century English high society. The names that have graced this stage—Julie Andrews, Marlon Brando, Katharine Hepburn—are the crème of New York and national talent. So these days, when famous celebrities of the era pass on, Lupinacci fields phone calls from the media, "and it's very rare that I say that one of them didn't perform here."

Ah, the grande dame! East Haddam is a gem of a Victorian river town, blessed with equal measure of charm, history, and culture. Its centerpiece: the **Goodspeed Opera House**, whose whimsical exterior is resplendently white, a wedding cake of glorious proportions.

Built in 1876 on the banks of the Connecticut River by shipping magnate and theater aficionado William Goodspeed, the Tony Award–winning theater still upholds its original raison d'être—preservation of the American musical. In the old days, theatergoers and actors were shuttled from New York via steamship to East Haddam, and you can still picture the ladies with parasols taking a preconcert stroll along the picturesque riverbank.

Today, the legendary tryout venue for Broadway shows (*My Fair Lady, Annie, Man of La Mancha*) with New York on their minds produces six musicals each summer (Oscar and Emmy winner Julie Andrews directed *The Boy Friend* in 2005), and develops new musicals at its second stage, the Norma Terris Theatre, in nearby Chester. In the works: A new 770-seat theater, complete with Broadway-size stage for larger shows, will be 21st century all the way. But outside will remain, proudly, a Victorian-era wedding cake vision in white.

Spin into Spring
Biking the Back Roads

Spring. The pavement is warming, and cyclists huddled inside all winter long begin to venture out. Last call for a spin in the country! You know, those two-wheeled rambles where you look out past your handlebars and marvel at the enduring allure of the rural landscape.

And so it goes in Connecticut: Must-ride back roads provide a labyrinth of possibilities that includes places to take the kids, leisurely pedals past old village greens, peaceful dirt lanes to recharge and realign your priorities, and leg-burning climbs and hair-raising plummets—if that's your thing. Cycling is a multiseason pursuit, of course, but spring, being as it is a time of awakening, is the perfect time to push off on a bike for an up-close out-of-car adventure.

Here, three to get your wheels spinning.

Cycling the Litchfield Hills: The Back Way

The northwest corner of Connecticut, oft called the Litchfield Hills, puts the *scene* in scenic roads. And what scenery it is: Every curve yields some bucolic expanse where old barns and proud colonials and 19th-century homes dot the landscape surrounding classic New England villages, one more lovely than the next. It's a county whose movie stars include the likes of Dustin Hoffman and Meryl Streep, where families have resided for

ANDI MARIE CANTELE

Connecticut's quiet back roads are perfect for cycling.

years and years, even centuries, and where the unexpected detours are just as intriguing as the final destination.

Few towns deliver on the promise of a back roads outing the way Kent does. Other than the drone of insects, the road was silent on a warm April morning as we pedaled past scruffy hillsides, freshly plowed fields, and crumbling stone walls, those handcrafted property boundaries marking the perimeters of long-ago grazing pastures. We rolled down CT 341 past country estates and old farms to Macedonia Brook State Park, where dirt roads head up into Sharon, a gem of a hill town. Back in Kent, Main Street has an energetic vibe compared to its toned-down neighbors, buoyed up by wealthy weekenders and a local art scene. We eyed the haute chocolate at Belgique Patisserie & Chocolatier, a classy confectionery in a renovated carriage house, then settled on Stroble Baking Company, where patrons crowd in for sandwiches and sweets.

North on US 7, the one-lane 19th-century bridge over the Housatonic River is one of New England's most famous covered spans. An off-the-grid dirt road named, aptly, River Road, follows the Housie's meanderings, with plenty of spots to relax and watch paddlers float downstream. Salisbury's Twin Lakes and Salmon Kill Valley are the kinds of places you doubt exist anymore, where country lanes are mostly car free, and 200-year-old farmhouses are set among lilacs and ancient sugar maples.

Finally, the hills: You gotta love 'em. No, seriously, especially for those hidden beauty spots that one can live in Connecticut for a lifetime without ever finding. Don't worry about the challenging topography, though—you'll make it. I know someone who pushed their bike up Tanner Hill just for the view of Washington's Lake Waramaug. (It wasn't me.) (OK, it was.) It's less embarrassing than you think—and you'll be grateful when a jaw-dropping panorama is spread out at your feet. My favorites? Skiff Mountain Road in Kent, Cream Hill Road in Cornwall, the aforementioned Tanner Hill. At the top, savor the feeling of having traveled much farther than you actually have.

Wish you stayed in the car? I didn't think so.

Suburban Ramble: The Farmington Valley Greenway

A passing cloudburst made the pavement glisten on the Farmington River Trail, a spur route of the larger Farmington Valley Greenway that threads through the busy suburbs west of Hartford. It was a chilly start, but the floodgates of spring had been opened. Sure signs were everywhere—robins sweeping low across the path, the scent of newly thawed earth, the river, free of ice, gurgling happily along.

An abandoned railway has a new life as a cycling and walking path—known alternately as the Farmington Valley Greenway and the Farmington Canal Heritage Trail, more than 18 miles in all through central Connecticut. As a route, the trail harks back to the early 1800s, when the Farmington Canal was an 83-mile, hand-dug waterway bustling with flatboats pulled by horses walking the towpath from Northampton, Massachusetts, to New Haven.

Multiuse paths are community gathering places, and here is no exception. For casual cyclists who wouldn't dream of venturing onto overcrowded roads, the greenway is a dream come true. The scenic route over

Crossing the Connecticut River on the Chester–Hadlyme ferry

easy terrain is a popular destination for an easygoing ramble or energetic spin. On weekends, when the paths swell with nature-seeking suburban-ites, expect traffic from parents with baby strollers, in-line skaters, and joggers as well as cyclists.

CONNECTICUT RIVER CRUISE

If you're looking for lovely scenery, the lower Connecticut River deliv-ers the goods. But you know what would make for a way more interesting bike ride? How about a jaunt across the Connecticut River via the Chester–Hadlyme ferry?

The historic village of Essex is postcard perfect, but you won't want to stay in town long, though. We followed the riverbank north past Victorian farmhouses and Greek-revival estates to Chester, an artsy village filled chockablock with galleries and bistros. Here, a ferry service has been shut-tling passengers and goods back and forth on the river since 1769. When we arrived at the landing, three cars were waiting in line; we paid $1 for the one-way trip (car and driver costs $3 each way) and pushed our bikes aboard the *Selden III*'s open deck. As we slipped across the river, we were treated to a spectacular sight: Gillette Castle, the fortresslike retirement pad of stage actor William (Sherlock Holmes) Gillette, perched atop the highest of the hills known locally as the Seven Sisters.

The soft green hills, the splinters of sunlight igniting the river, and the ferry's centuries-old pace conspired to lull us into lethargy. But we came to ride, so we climbed up to Gillette's fieldstone home-turned-state park, then dipped down into East Haddam, whose centerpiece is the 1876 Goodspeed Opera House. Back across the river on the antique iron bridge that swivels open for boats heading to and from Long Island Sound, we took CT 154—the old way to the coast—back to Essex.

What's the perfect way to end a bike ride on a perfect spring day? How about shad? The springtime shad run sparks a frenzy of activity in these parts, from Haddam's Shad Museum and Spencer's Shad Shack to plank-baked "poor man's salmon" at the Rotary Club Shad Bake in Essex, all in the name of good eatin'.

❋ ❋ ❋ ❋ ❋ ❋ ❋ ❋

IF YOU GO:

The state Department of Environmental Protection (860-594-2000; www.ct.gov/dot), publishes a statewide road map highlighting recommended local and cross-state cycling routes. Backroad Bicycling in Connecticut *(Andi Marie Cantele/The Countryman Press) features 32 bike tours around the state.*

❋ ❋ ❋ ❋ ❋ ❋ ❋ ❋

A River Runs Through It

The Housatonic River

Brian pointed to a splotch of ripply water near the muddy riverbank.

"Put it right in there," he instructed.

I cast the line 30 feet, dropping the lure right in the target area, the fast current behind a submerged boulder where a smallmouth bass may be hiding. After a few casts and no strikes, we whistled for the dogs and moved on.

And so went the rest of the day on the Housatonic River, the spectacularly scenic waterway that wends through western Connecticut. "There is no tonic like the Housatonic," Oliver Wendell Holmes Sr. famously opined, a pithy phrase that found its way onto many a tourism brochure. The American statesman sure had it right—if, in fact, it was he who actually said it (the same observation is also attributed to Thoreau, Emerson, and Twain). No matter: The people who live here, too, know they've got something good.

From its source in the Berkshires, the Housatonic, whose name is derived from a Mohican word meaning "place beyond the mountains," flows south for 149 miles, slipping past villages and farm fields and rushing under three covered bridges before emptying into Long Island Sound. But what makes this winding, rock-bottomed river so special? It depends on whom you ask, because there are many ways to experience the Housie, as outdoorsy folks around here like to call it.

Paddling the Housatonic River in Falls Village

In spring, when the river issues its siren song, and well into fall, the surface is dotted with all manner of self-propelled watercraft. Clarke Outdoors, a West Cornwall outfit, is the hub of river activity and sends visitors on excursions of every stripe: a laid-back drift in a tube, a paddle via canoe or kayak, even rafting through Class V white water in Bulls Bridge gorge.

Here's what we like to do: load up our '66 Land Rover, bribe the Labs, Maggie and Truman, into the back, and bounce along dirt roads right to the Massachusetts border. The dogs know this place well, and at a quiet spot where the river runs broad and flat between thick woods and cornfields, they're off like a shot, racing ahead as we lug fishing poles and picnic gear. Under a true-blue sky, we shove the bow of our timeworn Mad River canoe into shallow water that's dark in the early morning light. We paddle around one watery bend after another, gliding beneath low-slung branches and past drifts of purple loosestrife. We prefer the river's lazy stretches of flat water, where the dogs can swim and flush frogs out of

67

the shallows while we fish the riffles and lose track of time. As we head back, the Labs flick their tails back and forth as we drift along with the slow-moving current all the way to Falls Village. There, the Northeast Utilities hydro station is a favorite put-in for day-tripping canoeists, who paddle 10 miles downstream to Housatonic Meadows State Park through a pleasing mix of moving flat water and white water gentle enough for a novice to handle.

Along the way, they encounter one of the loveliest sights on the river—in all of New England, for that matter. The 19th-century red clapboard covered bridge in West Cornwall is a much-photographed landmark and a good place to enjoy a picnic or explore the village's funky assortment of shops and galleries (Ian Ingersoll's reproduction Shaker furniture showroom is a must-stop, as is the Wandering Moose, a friendly local café). Today, if you stand at the top of Main Street, mentally erasing the automobiles, the view down to the river is pretty much as it was a century ago. The Housatonic is also a superb trout stream, and the river's most ubiquitous sight is with little doubt the wader-clad anglers, oft seen reading the water and abiding the river's catch-and-release policy while casting flies and exercising their patience at hot spots like Split Rock, Push-em-Up and Two-Car Hole.

During hot, dry summers, the stretch below West Cornwall is rocky and shallow, so it's best to check ahead before planning a trip of any sort. Due to a federal ruling ordering natural river flow, or "run of river," the hydro plant no longer stores water behind the dam, the old "pond-and-release" system that raised too-low water levels for recreational boaters, or for power during times of peak demand.

"It used to be so predictable," lamented Jenifer Clarke, who runs Clarke Outdoors with her husband, nine-time National Canoe Champion Mark Clarke. "People could just come up and canoe or kayak whenever they wanted. Now trips are trickier to plan."

But if you come just for the setting, you won't be disappointed. The beauty of this place never ceases to amaze us, and on the drive home, the old Rover smelled like wet, happy, river dogs, and we relished the tonic of a day spent in perfect peace. River folks understand the energy that exists on the water, the peaceful rhythm of a river rolling on that pulls you back again and again.

❋ ❋ ❋ ❋ ❋ ❋ ❋ ❋

IF YOU GO:

Clarke Outdoors *(860-672-6365; www.clarkeoutdoors.com), 163 River Rd. (US 7), West Cornwall. Guided white-water raft trips on April weekends; kayak instruction, and canoe, tube, kayak, and raft rentals mid-April through October (reservations are a good idea).* **Housatonic River Outfitters** *(860-672-1010; www.dryflies.com) and* **Housatonic Meadows Fly Shop** *(860-672-6064) in Cornwall Bridge offer guide services and fishing gear.* **Getting there:** *From Hartford take I-84 west to exit 39, then follow CT 4 west to Cornwall. From Danbury take I-84 east to exit 7; US 7 north follows the river to the Massachusetts state line.*

In May, the **Housatonic Downriver Connecticut State Championship**, *hosted by the New England Canoe & Kayak Racing Association (www.necanoe.org), is the river's unofficial springtime kick-off. A colorful mix of weekend warriors and pros takes part in a spectator-friendly 10-mile race from Salisbury to Cornwall Bridge.*

❋ ❋ ❋ ❋ ❋ ❋ ❋ ❋

ON THE WATERFRONT

Mystic Seaport: The Museum of America and the Sea

A stiff wind blowing off the slate-gray surface of the Mystic River did little to deter the musicians on Lighthouse Point, who plucked at banjos, mandolins, and guitars, voices raised in perfect harmony.

> To Cuba's coast we are bound, me boys,
> Weigh me boys for Cuba;
> To Cuba's coast, don't ya make a noise,
> And we're runnin' down to Cuba;
> Loaded down with Georgia pine,
> Weigh me boys for Cuba;
> Load 'er up with sugar and rum,
> Runnin' down to Cuba.

Mystic is all about water. The seafaring town named for *mistick*, a Mohegan word meaning "tidal river," has been a sailing hot spot ever since the shipbuilding boom of the mid-1700s and 1800s, when some of the fastest clipper ships in America were built here. While you're more likely to see out-of-town yachties these days, it's easy to imagine a proud whaler pulling into the Mystic River after years at sea.

So who better to host one of North America's best annual sea music

Mystic Seaport: The Museum of America and the Sea

festivals than Mystic Seaport, the nation's largest maritime museum? Connecticut's star family attraction begs to be taken more seriously than your standard-issue tourist venue and draws 300,000 visitors a year to more than 60 historic buildings and homes on a 17-acre complex just a stone's throw from Long Island Sound. On and off the water resides the world's largest collection of historic vessels, including the seaport's show-piece: the majestic *Charles W. Morgan*, America's last surviving wooden whaler.

We drove down to the coast on a sunny June morning, lured, like thousands of others, by the idea of seeing and hearing authentic sea songs performed on gleaming wooden ship decks and beneath billowing canvas sails. This is the music from oceans around the world: sea chanteys, deep-water sailor songs, contemporary works, and classics from the golden age of sailing.

For those who made their living on or near the sea centuries ago, songs were a primary means of expression. Some were sung for pleasure, while shipboard work songs, called chanteys, were set-to-music tales of hardship and courage that helped accomplish the strenuous task of run-ning a 19th-century sailing ship. Aboard Mystic Seaport's tall ship *Joseph Conrad*, visitors plucked from the crowd helped raise a wooden lifeboat over the port side, their rhythmic singing keeping time as their hands turned the enormous capstan wheel. Around the village we heard whaling songs and fo'c'sle songs, also known as forebitters, the leisure tunes sailors sang for their own amusement. Haunting nautical ballads about life at sea echoed through the lovely Greenmanville Church, whose pews were crowded with music fans, young and old, who came from around the Northeast to hear songs of the past brought to life.

The appeal?

"People can rely on traditional music because it's stable, it's unchang-ing, it has roots tied to historical events and the lives of common people," explained David Littlefield, one of Mystic Seaport's own chanteymen. "In an ever-changing world, you can tap into that music."

In addition to a core of New England whaling songs, each year the festi-

✳ ✳ ✳ ✳ ✳ ✳ ✳ ✳

IF YOU GO:

Mystic Seaport: *The Museum of America and the Sea (860-572-5315, 1-888-973-2767; www.mysticseaport.org), 75 Greenmanville Ave. (CT 27), Mystic. Open daily 9–5 April through October; 10–4 November through March; closed Christmas Day. Check online for the current schedule of exhibits, activities, and special events.* **Getting there:** *exit 90 off I-95; the seaport is 1 mile south on CT 27.*

Just down the road, you can live out your marine-biologist pipe dream at **Mystic Aquarium & Institute for Exploration** *(860-572-5955; www.mysticaquarium.org), 55 Coogan Blvd., Mystic. Among the aquarium's aquatic residents: African penguins, beluga whales, rare Steller sea lions, and northern fur seals. Youngsters love the ray touch pool and the re-created Amazon rain forest. Dr. Robert Ballard's Institute for Exploration has interactive exhibits on the* Titanic *and John F. Kennedy's lost patrol boat PT-109, both discovered by the renowned explorer. Open daily; closed Thanksgiving, Christmas, and New Year's Day; call for hours and admission.*

✳ ✳ ✳ ✳ ✳ ✳ ✳ ✳

val includes music from the international maritime community, and the songs sung by Bengali fishermen on Bangladesh's vast network of rivers were a treat. The voyages of the *Charles W. Morgan* spanned the globe, Littlefield noted, "so those sailors would have heard music all around the world."

In the era when New England's whaling industry was booming, the *Morgan* was one of hundreds of ships sailing the high seas in search of the whale oil needed to fuel the needs of a rapidly growing nation. Since her maiden voyage in 1841, the *Morgan* made 37 voyages in an 80-year run, bringing in more than $1.4 million worth of whale oil and baleen, or whale bone. With her whaling career over, she retired to Mystic Seaport in 1941, where the 133-foot-long ship has been a telltale presence along the waterfront ever since.

On her broad, wooden deck, a docent showed us the tools of the trade—harpoon heads, lances, spikes, and knives—used for processing whales into oil. Once a whale was caught, its blubber was melted into oil in kettles on deck, then stored in some three thousand casks and barrels. It was hard to imagine how a 35-man crew could spend years at sea in the cramped confines belowdecks.

Mystic Seaport's signature exhibit, *Voyages: Stories of America and the Sea,* boasts hundreds of artifacts, paintings, and photographs reminiscent of distant ports, exotic far-flung destinations, and adventures on the high seas.

You can easily spend an entire weekend or more here, and that's just fine. There was so much left to do: a horse-and-carriage ride through the village streets, an excursion aboard the historic coal-fired steamboat *Sabino,* even a day sail into Fishers Island Sound aboard the 33-foot ketch *Araminta.* In the meantime, we settled into our new repertoire of sea music, humming chanteys, forebitters, and ballads all the way down I-95.

> Oh good Lord how the wind do blow,
> Weigh me boys for Cuba;
> Runnin' south from the ice and snow
> And we're runnin' down to Cuba.

LIVING HISTORY

The First Company Governor's Horse Guards

From my spot along the paddock fence, the distant sound of snorts, sharp commands, and hoofbeats pounding frozen dirt carried across the brisk night air. Suddenly, a squad of horses and their riders trotted out of the dark woods in a crisp line and, at the command "Troopers, right about!" executed a flawless 180-degree turn. As two- and four-legged members of the First Company Governor's Horse Guards went through their paces, I watched what appeared to be a page in a history book that came to life in a darkened field in the Hartford suburbs.

For folks passing through Avon on CT 167, the sprawling barns and paddocks are a familiar sight. And on Thursday evenings, visitors can stop by and watch Connecticut history of the equine kind come alive as the cavalry unit practices military maneuvers that date back centuries.

It's a headlong gallop through the state's military past that is reminiscent of the glory days of the cavalry, when soldiers fought, scouted, and raided while mounted on horseback. The horse guard is no longer used for military service; still, it's an arm of the Connecticut militia, and its 200-year-old history is carried forward by an all-volunteer group of 76 active troopers and staff members.

Sergeant Howard Miller, the troop's historian, filled me in on its storied past. Chartered in 1788 as the Governor's Independent Volunteer Troop of Horse Guards, the unit carried out its first public duty a year

The First Company Governor's Horse Guards

later: by escorting George Washington to Hartford during the general's summertime tour through Connecticut. Later, the troop provided ceremonial military escorts for Connecticut governors and visiting dignitaries, from presidents (Washington and Madison) to war heroes (Sheridan and Grant). In 1916, the unit was sworn into federal service and sent to patrol the Mexican border.

These days, the volunteer cavalry unit is strictly for show, appearing at holiday parades and state functions, presidential inaugurations (including those of Eisenhower, Nixon, Carter, Reagan, Bush, and G. W. Bush), and state fairs, even aiding the occasional search-and-rescue mission. In addition to the weekly drills, the public is invited to the troop's annual horse shows and open houses.

Today's training is still based on old U.S. cavalry traditions. First, new recruits learn the parts of a traditional McClellan saddle, then how to groom and tack up a horse and lead it onto the drill field, where they practice maneuvers such as those required for crowd-control formations, including how to form wedges and diagonals.

The U.S. cavalry peaked in the first half of the 20th century, and these days, only two other states—Arizona and New Hampshire—have active horse guards. So why, many people ask, does little Connecticut have two? It's a 19th-century tale of two capitals, when New Haven and Hartford shared the role. The Second Company Governor's Horse Guards, established in 1808 to escort Governor Jonathan Trumbull Jr. between the two cities, is based in Newtown.

Another change is who can become a trooper. In the early days, the guard's ranks were a veritable who's who of Hartford society, from Revolutionary War veterans to the city's movers and shakers. Today, the tradition is carried out by a cross-section of society. Little did I know that I was watching an attorney, teacher, landscape architect, firefighter, massage therapist, first selectman, corrections officer, legislative aide, and a field hockey coach executing the precise maneuvers on the field.

Recruits train for 16 weeks, including a stint at Connecticut's military training ground in Niantic, all the while learning about troop history, military protocol, how to wear the uniform, and whom to salute and when, in addition to how to ride and march—instruction that comes straight out of 19th-century cavalry manuals.

"The U.S. cavalry preferred people with no riding experience," explained First Lieutenant and Troop Adjutant Steve Ardussi, "so they could teach them the *right* way."

On this cold February evening, there was a flurry of activity outside the rambling red barn, as most of the troop's 35 brown, black, and chestnut geldings were readied for tonight's drills. I walked down the classic military-style picket line as members of the riding platoon, outfitted in olive-drab breeches, polished leather boots with gleaming silver spurs, and wide-brimmed hats, arranged themselves into squads and tacked up their mounts. Out on the field, squads broke up into columns of twos and fours and practiced walking, trotting—even cantering—side by side with barely six inches separating each horse and rider.

❋ ❋ ❋ ❋ ❋ ❋ ❋ ❋

IF YOU GO:

The First Company Governor's Horse Guards *(860-673-3525; www.govhorseguards.org), 232 West Avon Rd. (CT 167), Avon. Thursday evening training drills are open to the public; weekend events include an annual open house in January and open horse shows in June and October.* **Getting there:** *I-84 to exit 39; follow CT 4 west and turn right onto CT 167.*

The Second Company Governor's Horse Guards *(203-426-9046; www.thehorseguard.com), Four Wildlife Dr., Newtown. The public is welcome to watch weekly drills (Sunday afternoons or Thursday evenings; check online for schedule). There's also a horse show in July and an open house in August.* **Getting there:** *exit 11 off I-84; exit 27A off I-95, follow CT 25 to Newtown.*

❋ ❋ ❋ ❋ ❋ ❋ ❋ ❋

While they warmed up, retired First Lieutenant Richard W. McDonald offered me a tour of the barn, where the sweet smells of hay, leather, and grain mingled into a delicious earthy scent. The horses left out of tonight's drills stretched out velvet muzzles as we strolled by, and McDonald had a story about most every one. Jake, his favorite, is out on the field tonight. Casey, at 35, is the oldest. Deuce "has a nice gait but doesn't like parade drums." Coda is a big fellow, especially compared to Nippers, who is on the small side. "He's a good little horse, though."

Dedication to the troop and Connecticut's military tradition is key for new recruits, but around here it's the horses that matter most of all. In addition to carrying out two centuries of history, there's barn duty, which means that on weekends and holidays troopers are mucking stalls and feeding their mounts. When I asked McDonald what keeps him part of the troop he first joined in 1957, he shrugged and offered a simple explanation. "I'm a horse lover."

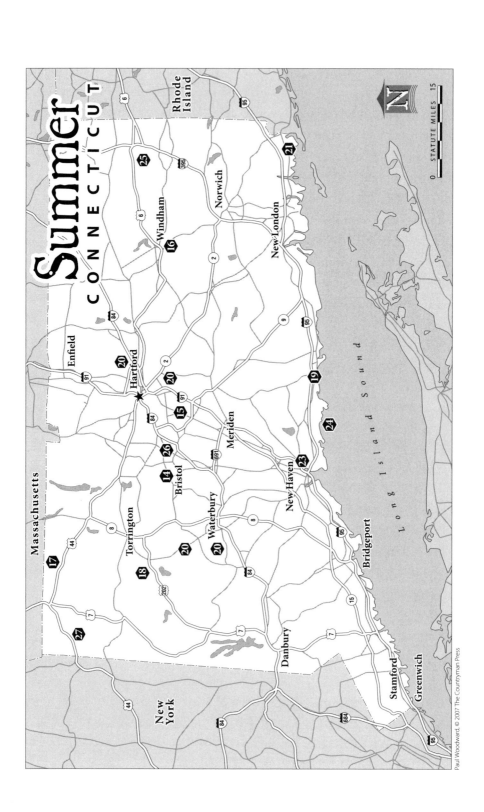

Paul Woodward, © 2007 The Countryman Press

Summer

THRILLS, CHILLS, AND HISTORY

Lake Compounce Family Theme Park

There are countless ways to while away a summer afternoon, but one of the best must be on a roller coaster, a credo backed wholeheartedly by Tony Reynolds, the man who spent six years riding the same one five thousand—*five thousand!*—times.

The ride is Boulder Dash, one of the top wooden roller coasters in the country, and the signature attraction at Lake Compounce Family Theme Park, America's oldest amusement park. "There was a 150-ride night a couple years ago—that was a good day," recalled the Massachusetts man who's also known as Coaster Tony.

So what is it about Boulder Dash anyway?

Wooden coasters hold a special allure that borders on mystical for many amusement park aficionados. This one, consistently top ranked by the National Amusement Park Historical Association, is the only such coaster in the world built into the side of a mountain.

When Reynolds talks about the ride (he has also ridden more than five hundred different coasters at every major theme park in the United States and Canada), conversation is sprinkled with terms like "great laterals," "side-to-side motion," and "negative Gs."

"You go up the side of a mountain, drop down and fly past boulders and trees, so close to the ground that you feel like you're going faster than you are," he explained.

PAUL FRANZ

Lake Compounce Family Theme Park is a cool treat on a hot summer's day.

Now, that I get. In this, the park's 160th season, Lake Compounce is Connecticut's premier destination for giddy summer thrills, but could it satisfy our grown-up amusement park appetite? One steamy Wednesday morning in June, Brian and I set out for Bristol to see what all the fuss was about.

The ground pulled away slowly as we rattled up Boulder Dash's wooden track. I reviewed the stats as we inched to the top: total drop, 145 feet; top speed, 65 miles an hour; ride time, 2½ minutes. We paused for a split second at the crest before, I'm told, I began screaming. Here's what I do remember: our car zipping past trees and huge boulders, screaming kids and adults going berserk with joy, and myself shifting between feelings of dread over what's to come and letdown when the ride was over.

The lakeside park draws more than half a million visitors every season with white-knuckle thrills and plenty of tame stuff for young ones—in all, more than 50 rides and attractions served up with a dash of history. The first visitors arrived by horse and buggy when the park opened in 1846 with a concert band shell, walking trails, and tenpin bowling. Lake

Compounce—"The Lake," as we called it back then—was where I, like many Connecticut kids, first rode a roller coaster. For years, I listened to the *whoosh* of rushing cars on the Wildcat's wooden tracks with a mixture of fear and awe on my way to my favorite merry-go-round horse before I found the nerve to take a ride. The 1927 coaster is still a Connecticut icon, and surely one of the only structures on the National Register of Historic Places that makes kids scream their heads off.

The 21st-century rides are more of the heart-thumping variety that bring passengers to giddy new heights. The big new thing this summer is Thunder N' Lightning, whose two mammoth arms swing visitors over the midway at 60 miles an hour. Their shrieks echo through the park, mixing with the screams coming from DownTime, a 185-foot drop tower.

I flashed back to my visit in early spring, when I was greeted by an eerie silence that seemed to engulf the 408-acre facility. "It's completely different than the park that people remember from when they were kids," said marketing director Tracey Blackman, as maintenance workers with tool belts spiffed up buildings with a fresh coat of paint and prepped the rides for another season of bustling activity.

✿ ✿ ✿ ✿ ✿ ✿ ✿ ✿

IF YOU GO:

Lake Compounce Family Theme Park *(860-583-3300; www.lake compounce.com), 822 Lake Ave., Bristol. Open May through October.* **Getting there:** *exit 31 off I-84; follow CT 229 north to the park.*

More Amusements

Quassy Amusement Park *(203-758-2913, 1-800-367-7275; www.quassy.com), 2134 Middlebury Rd., Middlebury. Open May through September. More than 24 rides and attractions include family-friendly rides, a water park, and swimming in Lake Quassapaug.*

✿ ✿ ✿ ✿ ✿ ✿ ✿ ✿

But I was thrilled to hear the 1911 carousel's Wurlitzer organ still booming, and the open-air trolley still clickety-clacking around the lake, not far from the Starlight Theatre, the art deco ballroom where Frank Sinatra performed with the Tommy Dorsey Orchestra. Today, it's also Connecticut's biggest water park, where an equal measure of kids and adults drench themselves on Thunder Rapids, a white-water raft ride, and Mammoth Falls, a 551-foot-long flume ride with a 50-foot drop. Our top place to keep cool: Anchor Bay, an 800-foot-long "lazy river" journey via inner tube.

In the end, we spent more time on Boulder Dash than any other ride. I didn't want it to end—a far cry, of course, from not wanting to ride in the first place. How did I get so comfortable? "You see scared little kids who get off and drag their mothers back into line," Reynolds said. "It brings you back to when you were a kid and you conquered one of your fears."

But to get the full effect, we would have to go back. "If you haven't ridden Boulder Dash at night," he said, "then you haven't ridden Boulder Dash."

And speaking of the dark, the park's Haunted Graveyard is Connecticut's largest Halloween attraction, a spooky, spine-tingling walk through six haunted houses and a ghoulish graveyard. It's all in fun—and benefits the Juvenile Diabetes Foundation—but not for the faint of heart. "For adults and brave children," its Web site notes.

At the very least, I thought, I could count on my own bloodcurdling screams.

TAKE ME OUT
Minor League Baseball

The lights that started flickering to life just before sunset were blazing at New Britain Stadium, where the city's minor league Rock Cats—the AA Eastern League affiliate of the Minnesota Twins—were hosting their in-state league rival, the top-ranked Connecticut Defenders (San Francisco Giants). It was a perfect July night: The smell of mustard and hotdogs saturated the air, and afternoon showers cleared off just in time for the second game in a three-day weekend series to go on as planned.

Connecticut's minor league teams fill a niche with fans who pine for the good ol' days of baseball, when the game was the pulse of the country. The crack of the bat and the roar of the crowd, after all, are woven into the fabric of our culture as surely as fireworks and apple pie, and still bring joy to the hearts of baseball fans.

Just for a minute, put aside everything you know about the big leagues—the multimillion-dollar contracts and shameless self-promotion. Now imagine a stadium with the charm of an old-time ballpark, an atmosphere that's part homespun nostalgia, part childhood memory, and, of course, part professional baseball. For not a few fans, the youthful exuberance of minor-league baseball is a refreshing break from the majors, and a throwback to a simpler time, back when cities were defined by their baseball teams and the stadiums they played in.

Connecticut is home to four minor-league baseball teams.

Twins general manager Terry Ryan watched players go through their warm-ups as the stands slowly filled with teens and families; on the diamond, swarms of little leaguers trotted onto the field with the team, while local schoolkids sang an out-of-tune rendition of the national anthem. "There's always something going on out there," an usher named Rich explained, nodding toward the infield. Up in the pressroom, sportswriters talked numbers: nearly 340,000 fans through the turnstiles last year, attendance solid this season, tonight's 6,389 crowd the weekend's second sellout.

The appeal?

For starters, fans get to see players up close and personal before they're signed by major league clubs. "When people in central Connecticut open the paper, they look at the Yankee box scores, the Red Sox box scores, and the Minnesota box scores, because they want to see how the guys they saw on the field in New Britain are doing," Bob Dowling, the team's director of media relations, explained. Francisco Liriano, A.J. Pierzynski, and David Ortiz passed through New Britain on their way to the big leagues; this season, the Rock Cats' bullpen has some top prospects, including four of the Twins' No. 1 draft picks (more than half of the Twins' current roster played New Britain Stadium).

"The stars of tomorrow are here today," he said, pausing to watch a homer sail over the outfield fence, our eyes fixed on the same distant speck. "The Twins draw heavily from the minor league. If players do well, they'll move up very quickly."

Then there's the price. Tickets at Connecticut's ballparks are in reach of almost everyone. A child's seat in New Britain's outfield stands costs $4; you can sit in the front row for twelve bucks (these days, I'm told, bleacher seats at Fenway Park are $20).

And in the minor leagues, fun is a big part of game night. Silly competitions and between-innings sideshows entertain those not interested in the action on the diamond, so kids who don't know a table setter from a backdoor slider are still in the right place. Children are plucked—with their parents' consent—from the audience to participate in contests, while others run around getting baseballs, caps, and other souvenirs signed by mascots like Rocky and Ball-D the Eagle.

"We do a lot of that stuff because families love it," Dowling said, "but we'll never cross the line and make this more circus than baseball."

Indeed, the just-like-the-majors moments—diving catches, RBI doubles, and other highlight-reel plays—drew the night's loudest roars. The Defenders scored three runs in the top of the ninth, including a two-run triple, but couldn't quite pull it together to stop the home team from a sixth-straight win.

In the end, it would be a big night for both teams. While the Rock Cats and Defenders sparred in New Britain, Giants slugger Barry Bonds would put homer number 714 in the books to tie Babe Ruth for second place on the career home run list. As I was swept through the turnstiles by a sea of jubilant fans streaming out of the park, America's national pastime seemed alive and well. The Rock Cats wowed a wired crowd, but going home, I'm sure, it would be the night they remembered, not the score or the stats. I recalled the words of Jacques Barzun: "Whoever wants to know the heart and mind of America," the historian opined in the 1950s, "had better learn baseball."

IF YOU GO:

New Britain Rock Cats *(860-224-8383; www.rockcats.com), New Britain Stadium, South Main St., New Britain. The season runs from April into September; game times are usually 6:35 Monday through Saturday and 1:35 on Sunday.* **Getting there:** *From I-84 follow CT 9 south to exit 25; turn left at the traffic light, then left at the next light onto South Main Street. The stadium is about 1 mile on the right. From I-91 take CT 9 north to exit 24, then the first exit for Willowbrook Park/CT 71.*

More Minor League Ball

    Connecticut Defenders *(860-887-7962; www.ctdefenders.com), Thomas J. Dodd Memorial Stadium, 14 Stott Ave., Norwich. AA Eastern League Affiliate of the San Francisco Giants.*

    Bridgeport Bluefish *(203-345-4800; www.bridgeportbluefish.com), the Ballpark at Harbor Yard, 500 Main St., Bridgeport. Part of the independent Atlantic League.*

    New Haven County Cutters *(203-777-5636; www.cuttersbase ball.com), Yale Field, 252 Derby Ave. (CT 34), West Haven. Part of the independent Northeast League.*

16

RED, WHITE, AND ROLLICKING

Willimantic's Boom Box Parade

You hear the parade long before you see it. The rhythm is so loud that it pulses through you. But there's the nagging feeling that something isn't quite *right*. And then the realization hits: There is music, lots of it, but no bands. Instead, the blaring sounds come from boom boxes (remember those?), carried by parade marchers, hundreds of them, all keeping time and tuned in to WILI, the local AM radio station.

Willimantic's Fourth of July parade is like no other, and thousands come to witness what is certainly one of the nation's most unusual Independence Day celebrations, and a beloved local event that maintains a great sense of humor about itself.

I never saw so many boom boxes in one place. Come to think of it, it'd been awhile since I'd seen a boom box, period. I arrived just in time to spot Wayne Norman, WILI's morning DJ and the parade's grand marshal. On this day, he's "King of the Airwaves," dressed in a purple robe, toting a scepter, and riding atop a yellow trailer outfitted as an enormous boom box. The crowd went wild as he tossed candy and bottles of water from his perch high above Main Street; behind him, the staging area was pure pandemonium as marchers and floats awaited their turn to parade through town.

In a corner of the state known for its quiet, this is perhaps the noisiest day of the year. While America has been celebrating its birthday with

Willimantic's Boom Box Parade is a July 4 celebration like no other.

patriotic pyrotechnics and small-town parades since 1777, the Boom Box Parade is a colorful local tradition that reaches back exactly to 1986.

It all started, as Norman tells it, when a band couldn't be found for the town's Memorial Day parade, and WILI offered to broadcast marching band music over the air on July 4 if people brought their boom boxes.

"We didn't know who would show up," he said, recalling the near-empty staging area hours before the parade. "I rolled my eyes and said to myself, 'What a great idea this was.'" But marchers came, boom boxes cranked up good, and a July Fourth extravaganza like no other was born.

Today, it's a famously free-spirited free-for-all that attracts nationwide attention, and like all great ideas, it has spawned imitators, "but none have sustained themselves, or come close in size," Norman noted. "Ours is a full-blown kind of thing."

Locals and visitors alike look forward to the parade, known for its creative entries and old-fashioned fun. Here, community participation means that anyone, from politicians to regular folks, gets a moment in the spotlight. The policy has had a curious result: In recent years, marchers have begun to outnumber spectators. "Why sit on the sidelines when you can walk down Main Street?" Norman said. "You don't have to do anything great—you can dress in red, white, and blue and walk your dog."

Of course, many do much more than that, and part of the fun is seeing who shows up dressed in what. I had to look twice when a Toyota Corolla plastered in road maps rolled by, a penguin perched on the hood. There was the Traveling Fish Head Club of Northeast Connecticut and a bevy of parasol-twirling ladies, a nod to Willimantic's Victorian-era heyday when a booming textile industry gave "Thread City" its name. The crowd cheered as each fanciful homemade float came into view, followed by clowns, fire trucks, politicians glad-handing voters, and a rollerblading waitress from the Willimantic Brewing Company handing out lemonade. More troupes fell in behind, sparking a frenzy as they make their way through downtown. Revved-up youngsters rushed into the street to retrieve tossed wrapped candies and colorful beads, squealing as marchers sprayed the crowd lining the parade route with water.

All the while, snatches of music drifted above the din as the procession moved toward Memorial Park. "We try to play the soundtrack of what a normal parade would be," Norman explained, which means standards like "Strike Up the Band," "Stars and Stripes Forever," "Dixie," and "Yankee Doodle." The combination of loud parade music and no bands conspired to make the festivities seem like a bizarre dream, one that didn't seem to end. After more than an hour, the dancers kept dancing, the marchers kept marching, the boom boxes kept booming, and the spectators kept cheering.

In the end, the biggest oohs and aahs were reserved for Norman, who, as grand marshal, is expected to raise the bar every year. Once he rollerbladed down Main Street, pulling a bus decorated like a huge boom box. Another time he rode high above the crowd in a cherry picker. "People pointed out that I really couldn't lead a parade from the air," he recalled. "And I pointed out, this parade has no rules."

As the years go by, more and more people participate, which brings about an interesting dilemma: Boom boxes, obviously, are critical to the success of a boom box parade, yet in an era of shrinking technology and a new generation of iPodsters, there are fewer and fewer of the hulking hand-held stereos around. "The parade doesn't work," Norman noted, "unless you bring the music."

✿ ✿ ✿ ✿ ✿ ✿ ✿ ✿

IF YOU GO:

The Boom Box Parade *(www.wili-am.com/parade.htm) steps off in downtown Willimantic at 11 AM on July 4.* **Getting there:** *Follow I-84 east to I-384 east (exit 59); take exit 6 and follow US 6 east and US 66 to downtown Willimantic.*

✿ ✿ ✿ ✿ ✿ ✿ ✿ ✿

THE SOUND OF MUSIC
The Norfolk Chamber Music Festival

As the Tokyo String Quartet launched into an evening of Beethoven and Brahms at the Norfolk Chamber Music Festival, I leaned over to my mom and whispered, "Why haven't we been here before?"

Looking for a dose of culture in a summer full of hot dogs, parades, and fireworks? This being the Litchfield Hills, how about music? Performances in the redwood-and-cedar-shingled Music Shed, home to the Yale Summer School of Music, have been a rite of summer for music lovers since the prestigious festival debuted in 1941.

Strolling the grounds of the Ellen Battell Stoeckel Estate, oft called Connecticut's Tanglewood, it's easy to see why. A patchwork of lawn chairs and elegant picnic hampers filled the rolling lawns, music aficionados enjoying a perfect August evening. At 8 PM, we filed into the historic hall to hear the famous ensemble, one of the highly acclaimed international acts that makes this one of the country's top chamber music series. A tradition of fostering musical creativity combined with its relaxed atmosphere and scenic qualities draws a loyal following to this gem of a festival that's part cultural enlightenment, part rustic Yankee charm.

"This is a big year for us," festival manager Jim Nelson told me, "this" being the Music Shed's centennial season, which has been feted with lectures, art exhibits, and free concerts by students, guest artists, and the

The Music Shed at the Norfolk Chamber Music Festival has been hosting concerts for more than a century.

100-plus-year-old Litchfield County Choral Union. Briefly told, the story began in 1899, when philanthropic music lovers Carl and Ellen Stoeckel launched the Norfolk Music Festival at their 35-room Whitehouse mansion, just a stone's throw from Norfolk's idyllic village green. What started out as informal musical gatherings evolved into a full-fledged chamber music series with the unveiling of the Music Shed, built in 1906 by New York architect Ehrick Rossiter. The Stoeckels arranged for special trains to shuttle audiences, as well as the top musicians and composers of the day, to their 60-acre estate. The invitation-only performances were attended by "1,500 of their closest friends," Nelson said (today the Shed seats around 700), while Carl watched quietly from the Shed's foyer and Ellen eyed the scene from backstage.

"It was absolutely no personal glory on their part," Nelson went on. "They wanted nothing in return. It was wonderful, just pure altruistic philanthropy."

When Ellen Battell Stoeckel died in 1939 and left the estate in a private trust to fund a summer music school at Yale, it came as no surprise, as hers was a musical family with strong ties to the university: Her father-in-law was its first professor of music and founder of the Yale School of Music; her Aunt Irene established Yale's first endowment for music.

Today's festival, which runs from June through August, maintains its original mission of presenting chamber music by world-class artists and ensembles and serving as a teaching facility for amateur musicians. Nelson's job involves recruiting graduate students for the rigorous and highly competitive program that allows them to summer in Norfolk, where they stay with local families and immerse themselves in intensive instruction. Concertgoers can take their pick: faculty concerts, Young Artists' Recitals (free and open to the public), plus some of the big names in chamber music, including tonight's Tokyo String Quartet, in residence here since 1976.

As the rich melodies of the Brahms String Quartet no. 3 in B-flat Major filled the acoustically superb space built a hundred summers ago, I recalled a little-known fact Nelson once told me. Unbeknownst to many

✧ ✧ ✧ ✧ ✧ ✧ ✧ ✧

MORE LIVE MUSIC

Summertime in Connecticut means music, and lots of it, at festivals and outdoor venues all season long. Pack a picnic and don't forget the blanket and lawn chairs. Here is an eclectic mix of possibilities:

Music Mountain *(860-824-7126; www.musicmountain.org), Music Mountain Rd., Falls Village. The music's the thing at the country's oldest continuously operating summer chamber music festival (since 1930), where you'll find the absolute best of jazz and chamber music, specifically string quartets.*

Talcott Mountain Music Festival *(860-244-2999; www.hart fordsymphony.org), Simsbury Meadows, Simsbury. The summer concert series of the Hartford Symphony Orchestra.*

Levitt Pavilion for the Performing Arts *(concert hotline: 203-221-2153; www.levittpavilion.com), Jesup Rd. (behind the Westport Public Library), Westport. More than 50 free performances most nights from late June through August.*

Charles Ives Concert Park *(203-837-9226; www.ivesconcertpark.com), Western Connecticut State University, Westside Campus, Danbury. A popular outdoor summer concert series with jazz, blues, rock 'n' roll, and classical music performances.*

Come summer, the smooth sultry sounds of jazz fill the air in festivals with a pleasing mix of small ensembles and big bands, including the **Greater Hartford Festival of Jazz** *(1-866-943-5299; www.hart fordjazz.com), Bushnell Park, Hartford; the* **Litchfield Jazz Festival** *(860-567-4162; www.litchfieldjazzfest.com), Goshen Fairgrounds, CT 63, Goshen; the* **Great Connecticut Traditional Jazz Festival** *(1-800-468-3836; www.ctjazz.org), Sunrise Resort, Moodus; and the* **Hot Steamed Jazz Festival** *(1-800-348-0003), Valley Railroad, Essex.*

If you're predisposed to old-time American roots music (think fiddle, banjo, mandolin), then bluegrass festivals may be more for you. The **Podunk Bluegrass Music Festival** *(860-291-7350; www.podunkbluegrass.net) takes place in East Hartford's Martin Park on the first full weekend in August. In July, the* **Pickin' 'n' Fiddlin' Contest** *(860-354-2912) has been a Roxbury tradition for more than 30 years. The old-time affair draws a convivial mix of locals, musicians, old-fashioned, and tourists to hear fiddlers of all ages play bluegrass and country and western music.*

✿　✿　✿　✿　✿　✿　✿　✿

visitors, the Stockels are interred at a quiet site on the grounds, and just before the concert began, we found it: Behind a wrought-iron gate, their unmarked crypt is tucked into the rocky hillside overlooking their Shed. Within earshot, I noted, of the lyrical sounds they loved, drifting up into the summer night.

✧ ✧ ✧ ✧ ✧ ✧ ✧ ✧

IF YOU GO:

Norfolk Chamber Music Festival *(860-542-3000; www.yale.edu /norfolk), Ellen Battell Stoeckel Estate, at the junction of US 44 and CT 272, Norfolk.* **Getting there:** *From Hartford follow US 44 west to Norfolk; from I-95 take CT 8 north to US 44 west.*

✧ ✧ ✧ ✧ ✧ ✧ ✧ ✧

STROLL THROUGH THE CENTURIES

Open House Day Tour of Litchfield

I don't often think of Litchfield as a tourist attraction, being, as it is, my town. Sure, it's as historic and postcard-pretty a village as they come, with stage-set architecture and a manicured green that draw tourists and well-heeled weekenders. But it's also where I shop for gas, groceries, and postage stamps. Come summer, an annual event puts an exclamation point on that day-to-day sameness, when we're all invited to sneak a peek inside some of the finest homes in a town famous for its fine New England homes.

If *House & Garden* is your bible, then a pilgrimage to Litchfield during its house tour should not be missed. The house walk—a tradition since 1947—is one of the oldest in the country and benefits the Connecticut Junior Republic, a 100-plus-year-old private charitable organization for troubled and at-risk youth. A mix of history buffs, decorators, and interiors nuts comes to indulge their inner voyeur or pick up design and decorating ideas. "But a lot of people who come are just looking for a nice relaxing day," CJR's director of development Hedy Barton said of the 1,000-plus crowd. Me? I love the mini thrill of walking through a private home that has ever-so-briefly opened its doors to the public.

So on this second Saturday in July, like every year, the self-guided tour begins at the tiny information booth on the Litchfield green. In this its 59th year, the Litchfield Aid for the Benefit of the Connecticut Junior

MARLA J. PATTERSON

The annual Open House Day Tour lets visitors inside some of Litchfield's oldest and grandest homes.

Republic, the tour's sponsor, selected six homes that Barton called "quintessential Litchfield houses" on the streets radiating from the green. North and South Streets in particular are grand avenues, lined with ancient trees and magnificent homes, impressive by anyone's measurement, built by sea captains and merchants who made their fortunes centuries ago.

Witness: The colonial-revival mansion on South Street, the charming Victorian with its original art collection, the shingle-style barn-turned-cottage with its sweeping western vista—we wanted to see them all.

First I joined the line of tour-goers in front of a meticulously restored 1829 mansion just south of the green. "We've been invited here for dinner a few times," the smartly dressed woman ahead of me revealed. "But it took the house tour for us to finally get here." We entered through a crimson-hued room with a glittery 1920s chandelier, an ornate Louis XV curio cabinet, and framed and signed White House Christmas cards. And while there was a museum quality to the interior, it had a comfortable lived-in feel. A tuxedo-clad pianist played a baby grand in the living room, which opened onto an airy Tuscan-style veranda. "Now *this* I love," a woman breathed, hand dramatically fluttering to her chest, as she craned her neck past the cascading pink petunias for a glimpse at the formal rose garden.

At Lane's End, a gable-roofed Victorian cottage with whimsical "fish-scale" shingles, we marveled at the panoramic views and unique original fireplaces. Inside the Heyday House, classical music played softly in the cottage's whitewashed potting shed–turned–kitchen, where buckets of fresh-cut daisies filled a table. Nearby, the Frederick Barnard House is still another classic structure, where men's and ladies' parlors, 19th-century paintings, and 10-foot ceilings evoke the elegance of a bygone era.

"The table is fairly new, but the chairs are two hundred years old," our docent told us in the dining room. In back, a brand-new gourmet kitchen comes complete with sandstone countertops, a massive Viking stove, and the original servants' staircase.

My last stop was the Sanctum, an 1820 Greek-revival structure steps away from the green; this was the first time in a century it was open to the public. The former family store, now a private men's social club, is full of original architectural details, from a Grecian window to fluted pilasters and a double-tiered front gallery. How many times had I hurried past the austere gray building, I wondered, clueless to its long history?

Not in town for the tour? No matter, since a stroll through the pretty neighborhoods surrounding the green is a popular year-round activity. Historic houses—colonial revivals, saltboxes, Federals, and Georgians—are everywhere, it seems. They are all private homes, but tucked among them are the nation's first law school and a fine local history museum, both open to the public.

And then there's the green itself, an inviting tree-shaded expanse sur-rounded by an architecturally diverse mix of clapboard homes and brick commercial buildings. Antiques shops, upscale galleries, and fashionable retailers mix with places like the Blue Bakery and the Village Restaurant that lend a homey small-town vibe. At night, windows throw a welcoming glow up and down the street outside. Nearby is the much-photographed First Congregational Church, a classic meetinghouse with gleaming white fluted columns and topped with a soaring spire, an excellent example of 19th-century New England church architecture.

How lucky, I thought, to have such a village to call home.

✧ ✧ ✧ ✧ ✧ ✧ ✧ ✧

IF YOU GO:

The **Open House Day Tour of Litchfield** *(860-567-9423; www.litchfieldct.com/cjr/tour.html) is held on the second Saturday in July and starts on the Litchfield green.* **Getting there:** *From Hartford take I-84 west to exit 39; follow CT 4 west to CT 118; the green is at the junction of CT 118 and US 202.*

The **Litchfield Historical Society** *(860-567-4501; www.litchfield historicalsociety.org) operates the Litchfield History Museum and the Tapping Reeve House & Law School, where local lawyer Tapping Reeve founded the nation's first law school in 1784, educating two vice presidents (Aaron Burr and John C. Calhoun) and more than a hundred members of the House of Representatives. Both museums, located on South Street, are open mid-April through November, Tuesday through Saturday 11–5, and Sunday 1–5.*

✧ ✧ ✧ ✧ ✧ ✧ ✧ ✧

Beauty and the Beach

Hammonasset Beach State Park

Ah, these lazy, hazy, crazy days of summer. A time of year when there's no shortage of things to do—weekends get booked, it seems, from beginning to end—and people crave the chance to spend time enjoying the season at the pace it was meant to be, s-l-o-w-l-y.

The ultimate lazy outdoor pleasure, of course, is going coastal and spending the entire day at the beach. With summer in full swing, so is the hot-weather action along Connecticut's shoreline, as Long Island Sound sparkles in the sun and public beaches are there for the basking in.

Mention Hammonasset Beach State Park in Madison and one image surely comes to mind: families with a gaggle of youngsters in tow and twentysomethings in tiny bikinis, all caked in suntan lotion and sweat and crowded elbow to elbow on a patchwork of beach blankets. For many—more than a million annual visitors, to be exact—the state's largest public beach is *the* place to spend the day, a favorite go-to spot for sunning and swimming. As summer heats up, the competition for those prime beach spots sizzles too (you may not get near the beach by late morning on weekends). When Lisa and I arrived on a sunny weekday morning in July, hundreds were already camped out on the two-mile-long stretch of sand, with just as many jockeying for blanket space.

"Hammonasset" is an Indian word believed to mean "where we dig holes in the ground," a nod to the eastern woodland tribes that grew

ROBERT GREGSON FOR CT CULTURE & TOURISM

Hammonasset Beach State Park has Connecticut's largest beach, along with a nature center and hiking trails.

squash, corn, and beans along the Hammonasset River. Colonists fished and hunted here for centuries before Connecticut residents started spending their newfound leisure time at the shore. Hammonasset first opened as a state park in the summer of 1920, and closed for a time during World War II when a federal aircraft range was set up at Meigs Point.

Come high summer, the beach is packed, but there's more than sea and sand to keep visitors here. A delightfully untrammeled wild side not far away is just right for picnics, hikes, fishing, camping, and bicycle rides. A 19th-century farmhouse–turned–nature center has hands-on exhibits, aquariums, and a touch tank for youngsters; outside is a butterfly garden, turtle pond, and small amphitheater used for lectures and presentations. While hiking along the Meigs Point Trail you can glimpse granite, gneiss, and other rock types; the Cedar Island Trail follows a boardwalk through the woods that leads to a salt marsh.

And while summer fills up and animates the park, the off-season has plenty of charms. When the beach crowds are long gone, birders come to train their binoculars on the migrant and resident species that love the rich variety of habitats. While ducks and loons float off Meigs Point, great horned owls perch in the cedars, and sparrows and snow buntings flit about in the thickets and fields.

For now, we walked the beach, reminiscing about a quarter-century of best-friendship and the summers that shaped our lives: teenage years spent on the Connecticut shore, memories of coconut-scented suntan oil, boys, and *Seventeen* magazine.

Isn't that what summer is all about?

✧ ✧ ✧ ✧ ✧ ✧ ✧ ✧

IF YOU GO:

Hammonasset Beach State Park (*main number: 203-245-2785; Meigs Point Nature Center: 203-245-8743; campground office: 203-245-1817; www.hammonasset.org), 1288 Boston Post Rd. (US 1), Madison. The park is open daily 8 AM to sunset. Meigs Point Nature Center is open Tuesday through Sunday 10–5 (phone ahead on weekends); reduced winter hours. The camping season runs from mid-May to mid-October.* **Getting there:** *exit 62 off I-95, follow the Hammonasset Connector to the park.*

✧ ✧ ✧ ✧ ✧ ✧ ✧ ✧

✿ ✿ ✿ ✿ ✿ ✿ ✿ ✿

MORE SHORELINE BEACHES

Sherwood Island State Park *(203-226-6983; www.friendsof sherwoodisland.org), Sherwood Island Connector, Westport (exit 18 off I-95). Connecticut's first state park opened on this picturesque spit of land in 1914; today it's the largest beachfront in the densely populated southwestern part of the state known as the Gold Coast. Its proximity to New York City all but guarantees weekend crowds in summer, but the spacious stretches of beach are lovely, the shady woods near shore are popular picnic spots, and some of the three hundred species of birds identified here can be seen along the tidal marsh nature trail. Connecticut's 9/11 Living Memorial sits on Sherwood Point, which served as a staging area for relief efforts; today a lone cherry tree stands in view of the Manhattan skyline, which can be seen on clear days.*

Silver Sands State Park *(203-735-4311), One Samuel Smith Lane, Milford (exit 35 off I-95). When the tide is out, visitors can walk offshore to Charles Island, where, legend has it, Captain Kidd buried treasure in 1699. The calm water (the island protects the beach) is perfect for youngsters, and at low tide, sandbars are dotted with tidal pools full of snails, crabs, and other creatures.*

Rocky Neck State Park *(860-739-5471), 244 West Main St. (CT 156), East Lyme (exit 72 off I-95). A 710-acre park with a white-sand beach, a stone pavilion for picnicking, and trails to a salt marsh. The 160 open and wooded campsites are available from May through September.*

Ocean Beach Park *(860-447-3031, 1-800-510-7263; www.ocean beach-park.com), 1225 Ocean Ave., New London (exit 82A off I-95). It's all about family fun here, from the half-mile beach and boardwalk to the arcade, mini-golf, nature trail, playground, and Olympic-size swimming pool.*

✿ ✿ ✿ ✿ ✿ ✿ ✿ ✿

GARDENS OF EARTHLY DELIGHTS

Come summer, gardeners are a busy bunch, deep in the throes of pruning, deadheading, and other dirty deeds. But even devoted green thumbs like to pull themselves away from their beloved patches of earth from time to time, to stop and smell the flowers in well-designed spaces by history's top landscape designers.

In Connecticut, 11 historic gardens are open to the public, reflecting a variety of design styles and time periods. See them all at once, or savor them slowly, one at a time. Our favorites:

Cities are different in summer—more laid back, more relaxed. Here is no exception.

When Harriet Beecher Stowe lived in Hartford's Nook Farm neighborhood, it was a community of reformers and writers (including neighbor Samuel Clemens, aka Mark Twain) that was lush with gardens and commercial greenhouses.

At the **Harriet Beecher Stowe Center**, our guide, Patrick, led us through the 1871 Victorian "cottage" that the 19th-century literary icon retired to, and outside, her beloved gardens, which appeal to history buffs, gardeners, and lovers of the written word.

"A beautiful yard with well-tended plants was an indicator that good people lived there," Patrick told us. But while formal, high-maintenance

A historic garden in full bloom behind the Webb-Deane-Stevens Museum in Wethersfield.

gardens were emblematic of Victorian-era prosperity, Stowe bent the rules: Her beds burst their borders in a profusion of bee balm and phlox, hydrangea (one of her favorites) and roses. "She felt closer to the divine in her flower beds than anywhere else."

It's no small distinction that Woodbury's **Glebe House Museum** boasts the only Gertrude Jekyll garden in the country, and the sumptuous borders surrounding the mid-18th-century minister's farmhouse are justly considered one of Connecticut's finest historic gardens.

In 1926, the famed British horticulturalist was commissioned to design a small period garden for the new house museum. While she never came to Woodbury, "she had a particular idea in her mind about what a colonial garden would look like," education director Judith Kelz explained.

Jekyll (pronounced JEEK-uhl) was in her 80s when she created the lovely layout, inspired by English cottage gardens and their informal,

✧ ✧ ✧ ✧ ✧ ✧ ✧ ✧

IF YOU GO:

Harriet Beecher Stowe Center *(860-522-9258; www.harriet beecherstowe.org), 77 Forest St., Hartford.* **Getting there:** *exit 46 off I-84; turn right onto Sisson Avenue, right onto Farmington Avenue, and right onto Forest Street.*

Glebe House Museum & the Gertrude Jekyll Garden *(203-263-2855; www.theglebehouse.org), 49 Hollow Rd., Woodbury.* **Getting there***: From US 6 in Woodbury take CT 317 to the first fork in the road; bear left to enter the museum parking lot.*

Webb-Deane-Stevens Museum *(860-529-0612; www.webb -deane-stevens.org), 211 Main St., Wethersfield.* **Getting there:** *I-91 to exit 26; turn right at the end of exit and follow Marsh Street to the historic district.*

Bellamy-Ferriday House & Garden *(203-266-7596), Nine Main St. North, Bethlehem.* **Getting there:** *From US 6 in Woodbury take CT 61 to Bethlehem; the house and garden are at the junction of CT 61 and CT 132.*

MORE GARDENS

For information on Connecticut's 11 historic gardens, go to www.flogris.org/cthistoricgardens. The voyeuristic gardener should pick up the Garden Conservancy's annual **Open Days Directory** *(1-888-842-2442; www.gardenconservancy.org), a guide to private gardens around Connecticut that welcome visitors. In Hartford's* **Elizabeth Park** *(860-231-9443; www.elizabethpark.org) at the corner of Prospect and Asylum Avenues, June means peak bloom of 15,000 rose bushes (900 varieties) in the oldest municipal rose garden in the country.*

✧ ✧ ✧ ✧ ✧ ✧ ✧ ✧

loosely flowing blooms. All her signature trademarks are here: perennial mixed borders with sweeping drifts of color, a vertical framework of shrubs and trees, and strategically placed benches for visitors to view the plantings from different angles.

Jekyll also liked serendipity, as with the delicate nigella (aka "love-in-a-mist") that pops up among the foxgloves and delphinium. "It looks like it just happens to come up somewhere," Keltz said, "which actually takes a lot of work to pull off."

Colonial America is kept alive and well in Wethersfield, whose historic district (Connecticut's largest) contains more than two hundred homes and buildings constructed before 1850. There's a lovely garden tucked away like a secret behind the **Webb-Deane-Stevens Museum**, but it's hardly colonial.

"Colonial gardens were practical," curator Donna Baron said of the plots that provided food, herbs, and medicine. "If you had a privy in the backyard, for example, having roses was good."

This one was designed in 1921 in the colonial-revival style, a reaction to not only Victorian formality, but the social upheaval of the Civil War, immigration, westward expansion, and the Industrial Revolution. "Americans began looking to their past to provide a base for the present," Baron said. True to form, landscape architect Amy Cogswell's design is nostalgic and romantic. A series of rose-clad arches leads to garden "rooms" full of old-fashioned blooms: Phlox, hollyhocks, peonies, and daisies share space with snapdragons, petunias, zinnias, and other colorful annuals. "Gardens were planted with flowers people remembered from the mother's and grandmother's gardens," Baron said.

Don't leave town without a visit to Comstock, Ferre & Co., America's oldest continuously operating seed company (since 1820). Gardeners can still buy seed packets and bedding plants at the original brick building on Main Street, where seeds are stored in turn-of-the-century tin-lined oak bins and packed by hand.

There's nothing so satisfying as seeing a plot planned long ago still growing strong, especially when it's paired with a historic home. The grand 18th-century mansion, home to Bethlehem's first minister, and later humanitarian Caroline Ferriday, is now the property of the Antiquarian and Landmarks Society.

But I'm at the **Bellamy-Ferriday House & Garden** to see gardens, so I head out back, where foxgloves, columbine, roses, clematis, and elegant formal plantings are in full unadulterated bloom (June is prime time here). I wandered past chartreuse clouds of lady's mantle and a profusion of peonies in well-tended beds. If you're not here then, don't fret: Garden designer Beatrix Farrand (who was, by the way, the niece of novelist Edith Wharton) planned for a continuous show of blooms from spring through fall.

A Fishing Way of Life

Stonington's Blessing of the Fleet

You smell the salt air even before you see Stonington's picturesque harbor. From the town dock the view is splendid. These days, you're likely to see more pleasure boats and yachts than draggers, but fishing here is a centuries-old industry, and Connecticut's last commercial fleet is still alive and well.

Here the workday begins before dawn, when diesel-powered trawlers and lobster boats motor through the early morning mist, out to where Long Island Sound meets the Atlantic Ocean. By evening, the catch of fish and shellfish is hauled out of the hold by weary salt-sprayed fishermen, sometimes after days spent at sea.

Historic Stonington Borough, a favorite among yachtsmen and weekending New Yorkers, is lovely: A quiet trove of antiques shops, galleries, bistros, and boutiques is tucked along Water Street, and narrow streets are lined with perfectly restored colonial, Greek revival, and Federal-style homes nestled shoulder to shoulder behind picket fences and well-tended flower gardens.

So how do you get a true glimpse of this working fishing village, just a stone's throw from the bustle of Mystic Seaport? Be in town, like us, for the annual Blessing of the Fleet, when Stonington prays for its fishermen and celebrates its seafaring heritage while remembering those who lost their lives at sea. Like similar festivals in Point Judith, Gloucester, and

Connecticut's only commercial fishing fleet operates out of historic Stonington Borough.

other New England fishing centers, the July event is part solemn remembrance, part festive celebration, where curious tourists mix with locals for a taste of the fishing way of life.

Stonington is full of sea stories, being tied up with the ocean (think whaling, sealing, shipbuilding) since it was settled in the 1640s. In the late 18th and early 19th centuries, fur sealers plied the South Atlantic, others got rich off the China trade, 21-year-old Captain Nathanial B. Palmer set sail from the village on the sloop *Hero* and discovered Antarctica, and Portuguese families started arriving from San Miguel Azores to fish the coast of New England.

When it comes to fishing, Stonington's go-to man is Arthur Medeiros, the retired lobsterman who remembers when his town was a close-knit, mostly Portuguese fishing community. "Some families here have been fishing for generations," he told me when we talked in the days before the festival, which he founded in 1954 with fellow fisherman Jim Henry after witnessing the tradition of a fishing fleet blessing in Europe during World War II.

Everyone, it seems, takes a break for the festivities that have remained virtually unchanged for more than half a century. Things kick off on Saturday with a New England clambake and wrap up on Sunday with the blessing of the fishing boats. In between, there are a fishermen's Mass, a parade, and plenty of authentic Portuguese specialties to be eaten. We wandered from booth to booth, sampling cod cakes, chorizo soup, *casoila* (marinated roast pork), and *malassadas* (fried dough made with butter and eggs).

On Sunday, a procession of marching bands, robed dignitaries, spiffed-up fire trucks, and Portuguese folk dancers wended its way through the borough to the fishing docks, led by a statue of St. Peter, the patron saint of fishermen. There, gaily decorated trawlers and lobster boats were called one by one—the *Sandra Michelle*, the *Miss Karyn*, the *Lindy Inc.*, Medeiros's *Seafarer*, the *Regulus*—to motor past the *Jenna Lynn*, where the Reverend Michael Cote blessed each vessel with holy water on their way out to the harbor. Out past the Stonington breakwater, pleasure boats joined the fleet as a floral wreath shaped like a broken anchor (a symbol of a boat that drifted out to sea) was tossed into the waves, honoring the 36 local fishermen who lost their lives on the ocean.

It's a poignant reminder that the future of fishing in Connecticut is tenuous, and a far cry from the heyday when fleets sailed out of ports up and down the coast. Medeiros hopes Stonington will continue to have a fleet to bless, so as time passes, the festival takes on greater significance. For many here, fishing still defines who they are, and most, like Medeiros, can't imagine doing anything else. After a half-century spent at sea, he's still down at the docks every day. "It's not like a switch, something you can turn off," he explained. "I wouldn't want to get away from it."

Fishing was a way of life for hundreds of Stonington men like Medeiros, but faced with an uncertain future, he says, younger folks are more likely to look for work elsewhere than take to the sea, a hard place to make a living. These days, commercial fishermen face tough federal regulations that limit the size of their catch and their days on the water. "It's still a good-size fleet for a small port," he said. "They're catching less, but the price of fish is better than it's been in years."

The festival was winding down, but we didn't want to leave this lovely place. So we wandered along the quiet tree-lined streets, past Captain Palmer's grand mansion, a museum operated by the local historical society, which also welcomes visitors to the Victorian-era stone lighthouse at the tip of the peninsula. We climbed the winding iron stairs to the lantern room and took in the 360-degree panorama of the borough and the harbor, where sun blinked off the water and the crisp white sailboat masts, and lobster boats pulled at their moorings. From this point, there was nothing between us and Portugal across the Atlantic.

Weekenders love Stonington, but it remains first and foremost a village of fish and ships.

✧ ✧ ✧ ✧ ✧ ✧ ✧ ✧

IF YOU GO:

Stonington's **Blessing of the Fleet** *celebration takes place in late July. The Stonington Historical Society (www.stoningtonhistory.org) operates the Old Lighthouse Museum (860-535-1440), Seven Water St., and the Captain Palmer House (860-535-8445), 40 Palmer St.* **Getting there:** *Take I-95 to exit 91; turn right onto CT 234, then left onto North Main Street and follow the signs to Stonington Borough.*

✧ ✧ ✧ ✧ ✧ ✧ ✧ ✧

PLATEFUL OF HISTORY

Road Food

There's no denying the summer pleasure of doing your eating outdoors, and whether your idea of perfection is a fabulous foot-long heaped with all the fixin's or burgers in a booth, Connecticut is a road-food paradise. Well-loved mom-and-pop spots run the culinary gamut, from cheap eats at breezy seafood shacks and old-fashioned hamburger stands to pizza joints and old-time drive-ins. No white linen dining or chain sameness here—this is sleeves-up cuisine, where you find a counter seat, snag a picnic table, or dine in the car, and be on your way.

Pizza, burgers, dogs, and ice cream are the staples that evolved into our quintessential favorites, and they're served up with a heaping side of atmosphere at eccentric old roadside attractions that transport diners back to a time when these one-of-a-kind treasures sprang up alongside the state's historic byways.

I was more than happy to do my fair share of research for this chapter (and received, interestingly enough, many offers for accompaniment). One thing became crystal clear: Which takes the prize as Connecticut's best depends on whom you ask. I unwittingly sparked many a heated debate over who makes the best hot dog, lobster roll, steamed cheese-burger, and Neapolitan pizza. Everyone, it seems, has a hands-down favorite. Read on and find yours:

Road food along the Connecticut shore

Sure, you can get a quick burger and fries at you-know-where, but why? The undisputed burger king in Connecticut is **Louis' Lunch** (203-562-5507; 261 Crown Street), in New Haven, the Elm City luncheonette that claims to have invented the hamburger more than a century ago. Forget everything you know about burgers, like ketchup, mustard, and buns: Here they're served on white toast and topped with tomato or Cheez Whiz. Meanwhile, epicureans and regular folks belly up to the counter at **Shady Glen** (860-649-4245; 840 Middle Turnpike East) in Manchester for cheeseburgers so famous, they adorn T-shirts. The technique is unique and universally known, and goes like this: Overlapping slices of cheese are added while the burger is on the grill. The edges ooze down and turn crispy before they're folded up into a kind of delicious work of art.

If there's anything more "summer" than bopping around town in a classic convertible, then I don't know it. So when we went in search of summer—and a decent burger—our vehicle of choice was a '57 Porsche

356 Speedster, top down, naturally. Our destination was just as summery: **Sycamore Drive-In** (203-748-2716; 282 Greenwood Avenue) in Bethel, whose burgers, we had heard, were some of the best around. We also heard they have car-hop service, which seemed too *Happy Days* to be true. But sure enough, a flash of the headlights nabs us a pair of Dagwood Burgers, which come "French cooked" (crispy edges surrounding a juicy center) and topped with every condiment imaginable. Happy days, indeed.

Weenies. Franks. Tube steaks. Red hots. Whatever you call them, you've gotta love the 2-foot-long Grote & Weigel-brand hot dog at **Doogie's** (860-666-1944; 2525 Berlin Turnpike) in Newington. Smother it with lip-tingling chili and sautéed onions, a squiggle of mustard, or, for purists, just plain, thank you.

It's a perfect night for paper-plate dining, being as it is summer, so we head to **Blackie's Hot Dog Stand** (203-699-1819; 2200 Waterbury Road) in Cheshire, a no-frills drive-in (since 1928) where the price is right and the menu is in line with our craving for comfort food. We cozied up to the counter and ordered hot dogs and birch beer. "Three! One!" our waitress calls straight back to the kitchen, where our Hummel franks are boiled in oil, grilled, and tucked into a side-split roll. Whatever you do, don't ask for fries. And don't inquire about the ingredients in the homemade pepper relish. That's a secret.

How can the name not make you smile? **Super Duper Weenie** (203-334-3647; 306 Black Rock Turnpike) in Fairfield started life as a mobile truck parked roadside. Not to be missed is the house favorite, the New Englander, smothered in raw onions, relish, bacon, sauerkraut, and mustard, made-from-scratch condiments on locally made franks. Down the road, **Rawley's** (203-259-9023; 1886 Post Road/US 1) has been a local landmark since the 1940s, where "the works" comes with sauerkraut, mustard, relish, and crisp bacon crumbles.

In West Haven, **Chick's Drive-In** (203-934-4510; 183 Beach Street) and **Stowe's Seafood** (203-934-1991; 347 Beach Street) have been shoreline favorites for decades and attract a diverse crowd: locals, tourists, kids in bathing suits, and Sunday drivers. Those in the know order piles of

---

From the roadside, classic prefab dining cars beckon the hungry and the travel-weary with piping hot coffee, homemade pie, and blue-plate specials. Connecticut's old chrome diners are bustling local fixtures that have a cult following and provide comfort like a lazy Sunday morning. In Middletown, Wesleyan students and workaday folks crowd into **O'Rourke's Diner** *(860-346-6101; 728 Main Street) for Irish fare, steamed hamburgers, and gourmet omelets and pancakes at brunch.* **Collin's Diner** *(860-824-7040; US 7/44) in North Canaan offers poetry nights and Lebanese dishes along with the blue-plate specials.* **Olympia Diner** *(860-666-9948; 3413 Berlin Turnpike) in Newington is a Berlin Turnpike icon with an encyclopedic menu of diner standbys.*

---

crispy fried clam strips and Connecticut-style lobster rolls (think hot, buttery chunks of lobster meat stuffed into a grilled New England-style split-top bun).

Clam Castle (203-245-4911; 1324 Boston Post Road/US 1) is a Madison institution serving up mounds of fresh-fried golden-crusted bivalves to throngs coming off a day at Hammonasset Beach State Park. When you're all clammed out, **Abbott's Lobster in the Rough** (860-536-7719; 117 Pearl Street) in Noank is a summer-only, seafood-shack sort of place known for its lobster rolls and lobster dinners enjoyed at picnic tables overlooking the harbor.

Ice cream makes you happy. Need proof? **The Big Dipper** (203-758-3200; 91 Waterbury Road) in Prospect is a perennial award-winner with an old-time ice-cream-parlor vibe. The older crowd indulges in familiar flavors like coffee and toasted almond (the house specialty), while the young 'uns go for M&M and cotton candy.

You know it's been a good day when your toughest decision is deciding what flavor ice cream to order. **Peaches N' Cream** (860-496-7536; 632 Torrington Road/US 202) in Litchfield serves up home-style ice cream freshly made on the premises in small batches. Here we're faced with a tempting mix of old standbys (cashew cream, mud pie) and seasonal treats (peach, red raspberry, blueberry).

There's no better cool down than ice cream, and if you're in Connecticut's self-described Quiet Corner, consider stopping by **WE-LIK-IT Farm** (860-974-1095; CT 97). Pomfret's traditional dessert stop is better than air-conditioning, and while you'll want to eat mountains of it, a simple scoop of the decadent treat is satisfying, tucked into a freshly made waffle cone or dolloped with hot fudge and whipped cream. The cows that provide the milk and cream graze all over the surrounding hills.

Pizza may have been invented somewhere else, but it's synonymous with New Haven, where pies come Neapolitan-style, meaning brick-fired and thin-crusted. There are legendary pies, and then there is **Pepe's** (203-865-5762; 157 Wooster Street). For newbies, I have three words: white clam pie. Frank Pepe hung his shingle on Wooster Street in 1925, and white clam pie (fresh-shucked clams, garlic, olive oil) evolved some time later. Like fellow neighborhood pie purveyors **Sally's Apizza** (203-624-5271; 237 Wooster Street) and **Modern Apizza** (203-776-5306; 874 State Street), the succulent aroma of garlic, sauce, and cheese lingers in the air, and devoted regulars happily brave the lines stretching clear out the door.

While New Haven corners the market on "a-beetz," just about every crossroads in Connecticut has at least one pizza joint, and many are well worth searching out. **Willington Pizza** (860-429-7433; CT 32) in Willington is a good stop when pizza pangs hit in the Quiet Corner. Many swear by the red potato pie, which caught the attention of the *New York Times* and *CBS This Morning*. In the Hartford suburbs, **Harry's** (860-231-7166; 1003 Farmington Avenue) in chic West Hartford center is known for pizza with pizzazz (think snow peas and organic tomatoes). After a day at the shore, **Alforno** (860-399-2346; 1654 Boston Post Road/US 1) in Old Saybrook is a must-stop for brick-oven pizzas with grilled asparagus, roasted garlic, caramelized Vidalia onions, and other gourmet toppings.

Serving Up Fun

The Pilot Pen Tennis Tournament

The timing was perfect: In the weeks before the Pilot Pen Tennis tournament in New Haven, defending men's singles champion James Blake vaulted into the position of top American player in pro tennis. The 25-year-old hometown favorite (Blake grew up in nearby Fairfield) was ranked fifth in the world and the tournament's No. 1 men's seed.

The state's major summertime professional sporting event brings young rising stars and top pros to the Connecticut Tennis Center for a week of competition (and $1.25 million in prize money). Pilot Pen is part of the summer hardcourt series of 10 major tournaments leading to the U.S. Open. And while there may not be the pageantry and unique grass-court play of Wimbledon, or the high profile of the U.S. Open, it's the chance to watch top players do their stuff on the pro tour, right here on the Yale University campus. This U.S. Open front-runner has played host to the best tennis players in the world, and the women's tournament (it became a combined men's and women's event in 2005) has always hosted a who's who of tennis greats—superstars like Steffi Graf, Jennifer Capriati, Venus Williams, and later still, Maria Sharapova and Amelie Mauresmo.

The weeklong event is equal parts tennis tournament and summer happening, with autograph sessions, a fashion show, live music, a rock-climbing wall, a fast-serve game, and giveaways galore.

Some of the world's best players appear at the Pilot Pen Tournament just before the U.S. Open.

And then, of course, there are the matches.

With seven of the world's top-10-ranked players, the women's field had some serious marquee power. Headliner Mauresmo was the No. 1 ranked women's tennis player in the world and the top seed in New Haven. The French player won the first two grand slam titles of her career this year, the Australian Open in January and Wimbledon in July. Then there's Justine Henin-Hardenne, the reigning French Open champ, whom Mauresmo defeated in the Wimbledon finals on July 9.

Finally there's Lindsay Davenport, the ace of American women's tennis who's returning to defend her title. The 30-year-old singles champ ousted Mauresmo in last year's finals; this year, she fought through a host of nagging injuries to return to New Haven.

All week long, the action on the stadium court was full of high drama.

It was all there: stunning upsets, close calls, and jaw-dropping shots. Early in the third round, Mauresmo was nearly crushed by No. 93–ranked Galina Voskoboeva of Russia before rallying to win five games in a row (but Davenport knocked off Mauresmo midway through the tournament and advanced to the semifinals). Despite a knee injury that had kept her off the court since Wimbledon, second-seeded Belgian Henin-Hardenne was a force to be reckoned with, making it all the way to face Davenport in the finals. And the biggest stunner happened soon after the first ball was tossed up, when Blake (the "hometown hero," as the local media took to calling him) made an early exit in a three-set loss to unseeded Spaniard Ruben Hidalgo during the tournament's second round.

While some big-name players don't want to compete in a tournament right before the U.S. Open—which begins less than 48 hours after Pilot Pen wraps up—others welcome the opportunity to play a few warm-up matches to tune up for the grand slam. It's also a chance to see the future of American tennis, like 177th-ranked player Sam Querrey in his first professional season, who reminded me so much of Blake, who last year was just a local kid ranked No. 186 in the world when he won the tournament and advanced to the quarterfinals of the U.S. Open a week later.

It's a big time for pro tennis. First, Andre Agassi, one of tennis's most dynamic and popular players, was set to retire after one more go-round at the U.S. Open. Also this year, the United States Tennis Association debuted Hawk-Eye instant replay technology, which involves a computer and a series of cameras that track the flight and trajectory of the ball to judge close calls on the court. Sports pundits say it's the most dramatic rule change in this tradition-bound sport since the tiebreaker was introduced in 1970.

In the end, Davenport and Henin-Hardenne vied for the women's title in what would be a less-than-stellar final. Davenport, who missed most of this season due to a strained back, was done in by a painful right shoulder that forced her to walk out of the final after only seven games, a mere 43 points in 25 minutes of play. The Belgian, ranked No. 2 in the world, was in top form but hardly needed to break a sweat. She beat the defending champion 6-0, 1-0, and earned $95,000 and the glass championship trophy. In men's play, Nikolay Davydenko of Russia easily took down Argentina's Agustin Calleri in straight sets, 6-4, 6-3, to win his third singles title this year.

For Blake and Davenport, the title was theirs to grab but got away. Davenport tearfully apologized to her fans when she walked onto the court to receive her runner-up trophy.

"I feel absolutely horrible for the tournament and for the fans," Davenport told reporters afterward. "Obviously they come here to see the best tennis. I just feel guilty."

And so it goes in pro tennis—in any professional sport, for that matter. And like loyal fans do, New Haven cheered her anyway, no doubt happy just to see her back in the game.

✿ ✿ ✿ ✿ ✿ ✿ ✿ ✿

IF YOU GO:

Pilot Pen Tennis *(203-776-7331, 1-888-997-4568; www.pilotpen tennis.com), Connecticut Tennis Center at Yale, 45 Yale Ave., New Haven.* **Getting there:** *From exit 44 off I-95 north, exit 45 off I-95 south, or exit 1 off I-91 south; follow Ella Grasso Boulevard (CT 10) to Derby Avenue (CT 34); follow signs to the tennis center.*

✿ ✿ ✿ ✿ ✿ ✿ ✿ ✿

☼24☼

THREADING THE THIMBLES

Scattered off the coast of Branford are islands where, in some cases, only one man lives, an island unto himself and maybe some seagulls. On others no one is in residence at all. These Thimble Islands share the scenery with cormorants and migratory shorebirds that pass through on their way to and from someplace else.

This oasis not too far from the madding summer crowds is home to a most unusual and exclusive Long Island Sound summer colony, and one of the great secrets of the Connecticut coast. It is precisely this exclusivity that has kept the islands off the tourists' charts. It's a well-preserved paradise . . . if you own one. Otherwise, outsiders need to know an insider. Don't have an invite from, say, celebrity residents Jane Pauley and Garry Trudeau? Do the next best thing: Simply hop aboard one of the excursion boats that take off from the charming waterfront village of Stony Creek, savor the salt air and the up-close look at island life, and rubberneck at how the other half lives.

So on a bright July morning we boarded the *Volsunga IV* to get a gander at this sweep of stony islets, and what a curious, eclectic, and ever-fascinating scattering of history, culture, and folklore it turned out to be. Captain Bob Milne regaled us with a well-rehearsed spiel (which, at his count, he's delivered more than 13,000 times) peppered with tales of pirate booty and island legends as we motored around Connecticut's

Thimble Islands sightseeing cruises are based at Stony Creek.

offshore gems, known around here as the Thimbles, whose history is unusually rich. To summarize: Discovered by Adriaen Block (of Block Island fame) in 1614, followed by centuries of bootlegging, farming, and quarrying (the islands' pink granite has been used in the Lincoln Memorial, Grand Central Terminal, and other American landmarks), then a Victorian-era playground so highbrow it earned the sobriquet "Newport of Connecticut."

"The islands are often called a piece of the Maine coast that broke off and drifted down to Stony Creek," Milne intoned as he expertly maneuvered the 40-foot *Volsunga* past reefs and tantalizingly close to the craggy islands named for the thimble-shaped berries that once grew here in profusion. The archipelago includes 23 inhabited islands scattered among many others ("If you count every rock that shows above high water, you might come up with a few hundred," says Milne). The closest are just a few hundred yards offshore and range in size from nearly 18 acres to tide-sloshed wisps of granite barely wide enough to support but a single house. Others bear dwellings of every stripe, from tidy cottages with fanciful gingerbread trim to shingled mansions with widow's walks and gazebos. Island life revolves around relaxing, evidenced by the prevalence of hammocks, swimming pools, and tennis courts. Regardless of their size, each has an aura of exclusivity that only adds to their mystery.

"Every rock that shows above high tide is covered by someone now," Milne said, and each seems to have a story to tell, with names that entice and tease, and pasts that are equal parts myth and reality. To wit: Mother-in-Law Island, so named for an overzealous meddler who followed newlyweds there on their wedding night and was summarily left behind. The 19th-century circus celebrity Tom Thumb was a well-known house-guest on Cut-in-Two Island, where he courted Little Miss Emily, a performer in P. T. Barnum's traveling circus.

There are enough references to Captain Kidd to all but nail down his ties to the Thimbles. They say his initials are carved in granite on Treasure Island, aka Pot Rock Island. Legend also tells that the 17th-century pirate used the lofty cliffs on High Island, better known as Kidd's Island, to plan raids on passing ships and dodge the Royal Navy. He stashed some of his loot, Milne told us, on Money Island, whose tiny cottage community once included a store, post office, church, bowling alley, and a hotel.

Of all the Thimbles, my favorite was tiny Dogfish Island with its neat-as-a-pin white cottage. Brian was torn between a windswept rock with a pavilion flying a black pirate flag, and the island claimed with squatters' rights in the 1970s sporting a cottage on stilts. Since even modest islands fetch several million dollars—a Tudor-style mansion on Rogers Island recently sold for $23 million, making it one of the priciest properties on the Connecticut coast—we would have to be content to dream.

As we motored back toward shore, other boats passed us on their way toward the Sound, including the *Night Heron*, dragging for littlenecks, quahogs, and cherrystones, and the *Charly More*, which ferries island resi-dents to and fro their summertime havens. Islanders start arriving in April, and by late October city water is turned off and they call it a season.

And how does a boat captain while away the off-season? Milne penned a book. *Thimble Islands Storybook: A Captain's View* is a collection of personal stories, island legends, and original poetry. He inscribed my copy with a simple yet universal message, whether for navigating the Thimbles or life itself: *Smooth Sailing.*

○ ○ ○ ○ ○ ○ ○ ○

IF YOU GO:

Stony Creek, the mainland gateway to the islands, is a destination unto itself, with a few shops and eateries, and quiet side streets perfect for exploring. Two tour boats chug around the islands, offering 45-minute narrated tours departing from the Stony Creek town dock (arrive early on summer weekends, as parking is limited). **Thimble Islands Boat Tour** *(203-481-3345; www.thimbleislands.com) with Captain Bob Milne aboard the* Volsunga IV, *and* **Thimble Islands Cruise** *(203-488-8905; www.thimbleislandcruise.com) on Captain Mike Infantino's Sea Mist operate from spring to fall.* **Getting there:** *Take I-95 to exit 56, then follow US 1 to the Stony Creek section of Branford. Pass under the train bridge and follow the signs for the town dock.*

○ ○ ○ ○ ○ ○ ○ ○

BLUE RIBBON FUN
The Brooklyn Fair

It's a cloudy and mild Saturday morning in Connecticut's bucolic northeast corner, and the Brooklyn Fair is in full swing. Early-rising fairgoers are milling around the grounds, and the weather, which vendors say usually ranges from hot and scorching to misty and cool for the weekend event, is keeping spirits bright.

The outside world ordinarily hears of this quiet spot only on the last weekend of every August, when the oldest (1849) continuously operating fair in America is hosted by the Windham County Agricultural Society on the Brooklyn Fairgrounds.

Connecticut's agricultural showcases are as New England as village greens and stone walls, and many have been traditions for more than a century. By the thousands, people turn out to watch teams of draft horses and oxen compete in the ring, check out prize-winning zucchini, try their luck at carnival games, and nosh on all things fried—funnel cakes, fried dough, onion rings, and other country fair staples.

It used to be that agriculture and New England culture and history were the focus. But more often than not these days, people are as likely to come for the live rock cover bands as the livestock judging. Many fairs are hanging their hats on a new era of entertainment and widening their scope to appeal to expected crowds, which for many of the state's top fairs number in the tens of thousands. At some fairs, the simpler days of the biggest-pumpkin contest have been overtaken by novelty events. A sign of the times: pro-wrestling matches, pig races, Elvis impersonators, American Idol–inspired talent shows, and on and on.

Despite a growing shift toward revved-up fairs, the 200-year-old organization that runs the Brooklyn Fair still banks on old-fashioned appeal. It's a formula that obviously works—*Yankee* magazine hailed it as the best country fair, not in the state, but in all New England.

It's an August tradition for many families—attendance hovers around 100,000 people over the four-day weekend—and while traditional favorites like cattle shows and antique tractor pulls remain part of the lineup, there are rather unusual and unconventional events thrown into the mix. Take Thursday night's Women's Skillet Toss, where contestants vie for the championship title by flinging a frying pan. What would a Connecticut agricultural fair be without women flinging frying pans? A lot less fun, that's what.

Organizers are not exactly sure why country-fair devotees, not to mention the folks at *Yankee*, love theirs so much. They can only go by what people say they like, and what the more than two hundred volunteers involved in the year-round planning think they're doing right.

"We try to be friendly," said Joyce Eber, secretary of the society, "and offer a good mix of vendors and events."

So one minute you may be in the cool, quiet confines of a display building with its exhibits of needle arts, honey, crafts, weaving, and floral arrangements. The next, you might be strolling a teeming midway, sipping just-squeezed lemonade and nibbling some of the apple fritters that are snapped up before they have a chance to cool. Later on, you could be hearing the sounds of foot-stomping entertainment courtesy of a country-western band.

Historians generally agree that the American fair can be traced back to Elkanah Watson, a New England farmer who organized a small livestock exhibition in Pittsfield, Massachusetts, in the early 1800s. Windham County's agricultural society, established in 1809, stands by its original purpose: Present an agricultural fair that emphasizes agriculture. Sure, a

CORY MAZON

Family fun at the country fair

few things have changed over the years. There's a 5K road race, and many of the photography exhibitors use digital cameras these days. But more than anything, the Brooklyn Fair stays the same. Take the country store and museum with antique farming equipment and a vintage kitchen, the piglets squealing in their pens, and the milking parlor in the cow barn. "We try to think of new ways to encourage people to come and see where their food actually comes from," Eber said.

In an era of rapid development, that's particularly important. Connecticut loses about 9,000 of its 300,000 acres of farmland every year, according to the Connecticut Farmland Trust, a preservation-minded private trust that buys development rights from farmers. There are 4,200 working farms in Connecticut these days, down from 20,000 in 1950.

Still, there are plenty of farm animals—donkeys and draft horses, sheep and swine, oxen and heifers—more, in fact, than at any other agricultural fair in southern New England. And the old-fashioned quilts, homemade jellies, and fresh-from-the-field produce still draw crowds, as does the fleece-to-shawl competition, a race that has teams using spinning wheels and looms to create a shawl out of raw fleece. Blue ribbons are awarded for two-crusted apple pies, polished vegetables, and gigantic pumpkins. Artists and craftspeople display their wares, sun-beaten farmers chug along on John Deere tractors, neighbors catch up with one another, and clusters of local teens huddle on the midway, where the Ferris wheel sends riders endlessly up to the sky and back to earth again.

A day finely spent, in New England as we dream it to be.

✧ ✧ ✧ ✧ ✧ ✧ ✧ ✧

IF YOU GO:

The Brooklyn Fair *(860-779-0012; www.brooklynfair.org), CT 169, Brooklyn, is held on the last weekend of August.* **Getting there:** *From I-84 east take I-384 east, which turns into US 6; turn right onto CT 169 south, and the fairgrounds are a half-mile ahead. From I-395 take exit 91, then follow US 6 west, then CT 169 south to the fairgrounds.*

MORE FAIRS

Connecticut's fair season starts in mid-July with the **North Stonington Agricultural Fair** *and wraps up with the* **Riverton Fair** *in mid-October. In between, August and September—the harvest months—are busiest. The Association of Connecticut Fairs (www.ctfairs.org) maintains an online listing of the state's local, 4H, and major agricultural fairs.*

✧ ✧ ✧ ✧ ✧ ✧ ✧ ✧

A LOFTY PERSPECTIVE
The Plainville Hot Air Balloon Festival

"**O**ur little prince came down from the sky and landed in the desert among us," Swiss Vice President Adolphe Ogi proclaimed in March 1999, quoting Antoine de Saint-Exupéry's classic children's tale, *The Little Prince*. The occasion: Dr. Bertrand Piccard and Brian Jones had just become the first balloonists to circle the world nonstop.

While the bravest of the brave shatter aviation records in high-tech balloons, the rest of us attend festivals, where we can marvel at the mystical flying machines, and those so inclined can climb into a wicker basket and lift off.

Afraid of heights? No problem, as long as you remember a few key points. Don't look down. Don't watch as the basket pulls away from the ground. Look straight ahead at the scenery.

At my behest, that sage advice comes from Mike Bollea, owner and operator of Windriders Ballooning, who hasn't missed the Plainville Hot-Air Balloon Festival in 22 years. What began in 1985 as a "balloon rally" celebrating the fire department's centennial has evolved into a wildly popular three-day fete drawing upward of 25,000 visitors. While firefighters cook hamburgers, hot dogs, and fried dough, balloon outfitters host tether rides, a nighttime balloon glow, and, for the brave-hearted, balloon flights.

"They think it's going to be like an amusement park ride," Bollea said of the first-timers he takes aloft. "I tell them that you don't get that elevated feeling like when you're on a Ferris wheel; it's smooth and slow."

There are many things about hot-air ballooning that scare me, I admitted to Bollea, from the lofty heights on down.

"In ten to fifteen minutes, you'd be talking to everyone and looking at dogs running around on the ground," Bollea reassured me, then added, "It's not like you're up on a ladder, you know. You're surrounded by a basket."

True enough. Nevertheless, a balloon rising gently into the air and drifting over the landscape is a moving sight to behold—from the ground, at least in my book. And my time on the ground, as it turned out, was well spent.While the gigantic shrouds—more than 30 of them, it seemed—lay limp on the field, their pilots were eager to chat.

Add a propane burner, high-tech materials, and lots of safety features, and the basic 18th-century design still stands from back when Joseph and Jacques Montgolfier developed a hot-air balloon fueled by burning manure and straw. The inaugural flight—whose passengers included a rooster, sheep, and a duck (who all survived, by the way)—lasted around eight minutes.

With three basic parts—envelope, basket, and burner—the anatomy of a hot-air balloon is amazingly simple. How the pilot controls altitude and vertical speed is a matter of basic aeronautics: The hot air filling the envelope is less dense than the cold air surrounding it, resulting in lift, or what makes the balloon rise into the air. The envelope, the part of the balloon that looks like a balloon (pilots call it "the bag"), is woven from panels of fire-resistant nylon coated in polyurethane connected to an open-air rattan basket with stainless-steel suspension cables. When the balloon touches down, the wicker acts like a shock absorber and the rigid aluminum frame keeps the basket upright.

I walked up to a candy-colored balloon just as its pilot light ignited the vapor, sending a 6- to 8-foot flame into the envelope with a loud *whoosh*. The pilot pointed to the top, where a vent, or crown, allows hot air to escape and make the balloon descend. Intermittent blasts of propane during the flight keep the temperature—and the altitude—

Balloons preparing to take flight over central Connecticut

steady. Upon landing, he said, a pull on the red rip line causes hot air to rush out and the envelope to instantly deflate.

Armed with that knowledge, and trusting the wonders of technology, I put out a contract: Someday, most likely, I would probably go up in one. Better yet, maybe I'd take one of the festival's tethered rides: A balloon is chained to the ground, and a winch reels you in when your five minutes are up, eliminating any worries about drifting far and away. There's even an inflated balloon resting on its side for people to walk around in. For $1 (proceeds benefit the fire department), the ultra-timid get an up-close balloon experience without, literally, leaving the ground.

As six o'clock drew near, ribbons of flame began billowing from heaters, nylon began to inflate, and the balloons—including Bollea's burgundy, red, and orange number—puffed out like enormous lightbulbs. In one of them, a silver-haired woman was the last passenger into the basket. At almost 90, she was making her first trip in a balloon, and she dreamily recalled the experience of another maiden voyage—aboard the *Queen Mary.*

One by one balloons lifted off the ground, each hovering over the crowd for a few moments before gently drifting away toward the northeast, skimming over treetops and suburban backyards. Balloons, of course, travel in whatever direction the winds blow, so we wondered aloud where they would land. Farmington? Avon? Simsbury? Speculation was still rippling through the crowd as the globe-shaped silhouettes became mere specks in the sky and then were gone.

I thought of billionaire British balloonist Richard Branson's much-publicized flight across the Pacific, and how, after an exhaustive preflight safety briefing, he jotted one reminder into his notepad. "Keep the fire burning," he wrote. "That's all that matters."

IF YOU GO:

The **Plainville Hot Air Balloon Festival** *takes place in Norton Park, CT 177, Plainville.* **Getting there:** *From Hartford take I-84 west to exit 32; head north on CT 10, then turn left onto CT 177. Norton Park is on the left.*

Want to float over Connecticut in a hot-air balloon? The **Connecticut Lighter Than Air Society** *(www.lighterthanair.org) maintains an online directory of hot-air balloon outfitters that offer sightseeing flights in Connecticut.*

ROAD ART
Lime Rock Park Vintage Festival

The man directing cars onto the racetrack was puzzled. "Shouldn't this be covered in mud?" he asked as he leaned toward my open window. "Safari vehicles aren't supposed to be clean."

Our 1966 Land Rover Series IIA was one in a long line of classic vehicles being marshaled into place at Lime Rock Park. With its rolled-up canvas top and hood-mounted spare, it was perhaps the most utilitarian entry, a workhorse among thoroughbreds. To the best of our knowledge it has never seen the African bush—just the occasional off-road outing in Connecticut—but it cleans up good, especially for the Rolex Vintage Festival, a showplace for some of the best dream rides you've ever seen your reflection in.

Who hasn't had the dream, the one about unleashing your inner James Bond, racing through the Swiss Alps in 007's Aston Martin DB5? The fantasy is alive and well when hundreds of classic cars roll into northwest Connecticut on Labor Day weekend. The festival, as its name suggests, features historic automobiles both for speed and for show. The sound of vintage racing engines echoing through the Litchfield Hills attracts thousands of collectors and enthusiasts who come from all over the Northeast to take in the races. Like always, the event's 24th gathering boasted three days of racing and a show displaying a select group of antique machines dating back to the early 20th century.

S. ANDRE YODER HARRIS

Vintage cars race around Lime Rock's famous 1.53 mile road course.

Any time a group of classic autos lines up, you're bound to attract a crowd, and festival's Sunday in the Park is no exception. Classic-car fans mill around the open paddock as owners proudly motor their lovingly restored babies into place along the track, and those bored with today's melting pot sameness (think ho-hum SUVs and crossover minivans) relish the peek back to the days when cars didn't all look alike. They're all here: Astons, Jags, 'Vettes, elegant beauties like prewar Bugattis and Packards, powerful Shelby GTs, sleek Mustang Fastbacks, Alfa Romeos (think Dustin Hoffman in *The Graduate*), sporty convertibles—Triumphs, Sting Rays, Speedsters—and the muscle cars of the 1960s and '70s. Visitors wandered among the cars and chatted with owners, some discussing the merits of overhead-cam engines, torque, and gross output, others just gazing in quiet admiration.

Italian automakers were well represented. We spotted not one, not two, but three blood-red Ferraris. A small crowd gathered as one owner recalled a visit to the Ferrari factory in Maranello and meeting Enzo Ferrari before his death in 1988. "*Molto bene*," the stylishly dressed woman next to me said to her husband, nodding appreciatively toward the prancing horse, Ferrari's racing logo. "The Italians have got it going on."

We saw great old cars otherwise found only in museums and photographs, and "daily drivers" used by commuting nine-to-fivers. What constitutes the pinnacle of automotive art depends, of course, on whom you ask. For some, it's the long, low profile of a Lamborghini; for others, the boxy toughness of a working machine like a Land Rover. People who swarm around our sand-colored Landy love the rhino-hide seats, the individually operated wiper blades, and the metal grill that can, in a pinch, be used as a cooking grate over an open fire.

Vintage auto racing on Lime Rock's famous 1.53-mile road course is much more than a high-speed parade of old cars. The flat-out, no-holds-barred competition is reminiscent of the good old days of road racing and puts an exclamation point on the weekend. We were thrilled to see the old beauties taking the turns: among them, a 1926 Bugatti T-35B, a 1931 Morgan Super, a 1957 Porsche 356, a 1962 Ferrari 250 GTO, and a 1965 Shelby GT-350. I couldn't help but think about the film *Bullitt*, and Steve McQueen racing his 1968 Mustang GT-390 through the streets of San Francisco in what's considered one of the greatest silver screen chase scenes of all time.

And there was more: a fleet of 449 Minis, fresh off a cross-country rally that began in Monterey, California; BMW motorcycle stunt rider Jean-Pierre Goy wowing the crowd; and internationally known automobile journalist Chris Economaki signing his new book, *Let 'Em All Go!: The Story of Auto Racing by the Man Who Was There*, and reminiscing about the days when he called races at Lime Rock in the 1950s.

The racetrack—one of the oldest continuously operating road-racing courses in America—is also home to the Skip Barber Racing School, which puts speed junkies in the driver's seat. And unlike, say, the Indianapolis Motor Speedway, where 250,000 race fans fill the largest stadium in the world, here spectators spread picnic blankets on the grassy slopes above the track and get close to the cars and drivers on the infield. The most famous person ever to climb into a stock car here is perhaps Hollywood icon (and longtime Connecticut resident) Paul Newman, who makes an occasional appearance on the track.

While we won't be in a position to buy one of the rarities on display anytime soon, we enjoyed the chance to ogle them up close, and commiserate with fellow owners about the electrical gremlins that haunt English cars. Our Rover's headlights sputter out from time to time on dark back roads, and the horn beeps on its own—in other words, it's British through and through. We got behind the wheel of our dreams and headed home.

✧ ✧ ✧ ✧ ✧ ✧ ✧ ✧

IF YOU GO:

Lime Rock Park *(860-435-5000, 1-800-722-3577; www.limerock.com), 497 Lime Rock Rd. (CT 112), in the Lime Rock section of Lakeville. The Vintage Festival is held on Labor Day weekend, but races and special events take place from May through October.* **Getting there:** *From Danbury follow US 7 north to CT 112 west; the main entrance is past the track office on White Hollow Road.*

✧ ✧ ✧ ✧ ✧ ✧ ✧ ✧

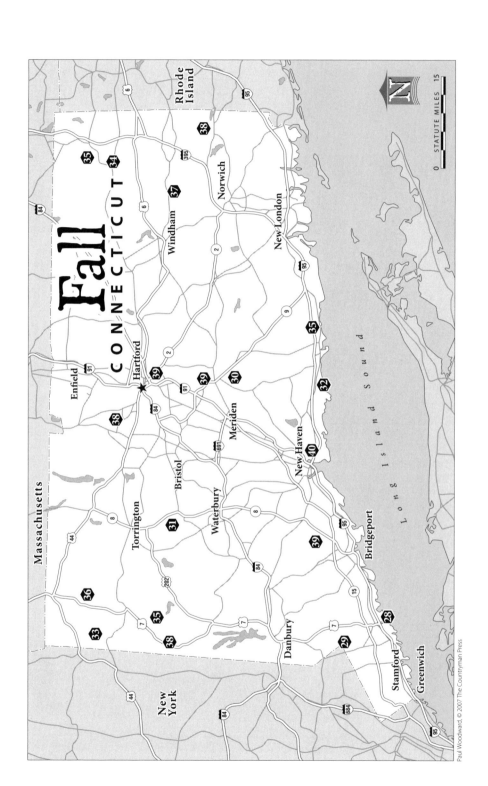

Fall

FUN ON THE HALF SHELL

The Norwalk Seaport Association Oyster Festival

"**H**e was a bold man," the 18th-century satirist Jonathan Swift once observed, "that first ate an oyster."

Whether that individual was bold or really hungry, one can only speculate. And whether oysters are a luscious delicacy or just plain icky is a matter of taste (of course, there's the aphrodisiac rep traced to Casanova, who purportedly ate 50 a day). Either way, the unpretentious-looking bivalve in the craggy gray shell has been a culinary favorite among epicures and the common man for ages. And like waterfront communities up and down the East Coast that host oyster festivals every fall, Norwalk lures oyster-frenzied visitors and locals with its Seaport Association's lively annual celebration of the Eastern, or Atlantic, oyster. It happens to be Connecticut's official state shellfish, more than 67,000 acres of which are cultivated in the cold coastal waters of Long Island Sound.

A small group of residents launched the family-friendly waterfront festival in 1978, and it has since grown into a key fund-raiser for local charities; the proceeds also help fund the maintenance and restoration of the association's 19th-century granite lighthouse in the Norwalk Islands. Historical exhibits give visitors a look at the world of oystering, which has flourished here since the 1700s; live music, arts and crafts, parachuting skydivers, boat tours, and children's entertainment keep things firmly

NORWALK SEAPORT ASSOCIATION

Oysters star at the Norwalk Seaport Association Oyster Festival.

rooted in the present. And while the three-day event brings all kinds of fun, the little mollusks are really what it's all about. So while the '80s rock band Asia jammed on the main stage, crowds lined up to eat oysters— batter-fried, steamed, simmered into chowder, or—for purists—raw on the half shell.

145

Let me begin by saying that my own experience with *Crassostrea vir-ginica* dates back exactly three years, when I pulled up a stool in Boston's venerable Union Oyster House one hot July afternoon and summoned the nerve to swallow a blue point. While the plump grayish-beige meat and its "liquor," or natural juice, didn't exactly thrill my taste buds, it was certainly interesting (the Corona chaser helped, no doubt).

But now I was worried. Folklore has it that one must eat oysters only in months containing the letter *r*, I overheard several times at the festival. Not so, a shucker in heavy-duty neoprene gloves reassured me. Refrigeration has made them a year-round food, he said, noting that raw ones are best in the cool months, after the summer spawn that leaves them plump and tender. And while he rocked his shucking knife back and forth to sever the strong adductor muscles oysters use to stay closed, he debunked another old myth, the one about a grain of sand morphing into a pearl. The real story goes something like this: A parasitic organism invading an oyster's salty home triggers the secretion of nacre (what we call mother-of-pearl), which coats the irritating intruder and forms the beloved, lustrous gem.

Wellfleet or Chincoteague, Blue Point or Belon, people can get snobby when it comes to oysters, whose meat tastes more or less salty and ranges in texture from firm to tender. There's plenty of archaeological evidence that Native Americans supped on them in southern New England for 4,000 years, fashioning the shells into jewelry, tools, and currency. Later on, settlers, too, devoured the mollusks, a staple food in colonial Connecticut. By the late 1800s, Norwalk was home to the world's largest fleet of steam-powered oyster boats; today, out past the festival grounds where the Norwalk River spills into the harbor, vessels head out before sunrise to work the cultivated beds, returning in the afternoon loaded down with bushels of oysters. The "farming" of the sea is called aquaculture, and Connecticut ranks sixth in the country for oyster production, according to the state Department of Agriculture. Of the millions of microscopic eggs females release during the summertime spawn, the ones that evolve into larvae, or "spat," settle onto the bottom of the sea, where they grow for about four years. Then, local companies like third-generation Hillard Bloom Shellfish, and Talmadge Bros., one of New England's largest oyster suppliers, harvest the bounty that the sea provides.

A short stroll away from Veterans Memorial Park is trendy South Norwalk, which locals call SoNo. The compact zone of brick warehouses was destined to become just another gritty waterfront neighborhood that time forgot before a reversal of fortunes gave it a new lease on life as one of Connecticut's most exciting hangouts. Though not quite as chic as SoHo, SoNo (just an hour or so northeast of Manhattan, by the way) has some of the same ingredients and is getting hipper by the year. There's no shortage of coolness on Washington Street, the historic avenue where live music spills from bars, and boutiques, art galleries, and culinary hot spots fill smartened-up 19th-century row houses. Families love the Maritime Aquarium at Norwalk, but here's what we like to do: stop by Chocopologie, a haven for chocolate addicts, then linger at a sidewalk café before navigating the throngs of scenesters at The Loft, the upscale martini lounge known for exotic libations and the late-night crush to see and be seen.

If SoNo was an oyster, its pearl might well be Bistro du Soleil, a gem of a place that transforms the denizens of the deep into sublime gourmet inventions. Oysters are on menus everywhere, it seems, from SoNo Seaport Seafood to the raw bar at the South Beach–inspired Ocean Drive, where they shine at their simple, elegant best—on the half shell.

IF YOU GO:

The **Norwalk Seaport Association Oyster Festival** *(203-838-9444; www.seaport.org) at Veterans Memorial Park in East Norwalk is held on the first weekend after Labor Day. Check the Web site for information on boat trips to the Sheffield Island lighthouse.* **Getting there:** *exit 13 or 16 off I-95; follow signs to festival parking areas. From Danbury follow US 7 to I-95 northbound.*

WHERE THE LANDSCAPE IS ART

Weir Farm National Historic Site

As you stand on the worn floorboards of his 19th-century studio, it seems as if Julian Alden Weir might stroll through the open doorway at any moment.

He might well have, a century ago. While his easel, modeling stand, etching press, brushes—even his rattan fishing creel—are at the ready, the American impressionist painter died in 1919, and his beloved farm is now part of Weir Farm National Historic Site, Connecticut's only property in the National Park System and the only national park in the country devoted to American painting.

Artistic types have long found inspiration in our fair state, so it's fitting that the hilly farmland whose natural beauty lured the likes of Childe Hassam, John Twachtman, and Albert Pinkham Ryder is now a refuge for nature lovers and artists, and a must-see for American impressionism enthusiasts. In 1882, Weir swapped $10 and a still-life painting valued at $560 for 153 rural hilltop acres in the Branchville section of Wilton. He wanted a summer retreat from New York City, and on his first visit he painted a small watercolor of the farm, the first of hundreds of drawings, paintings, and prints to come. The farm became not only his muse, but something of an artists' colony. "The Land of Nod" is what Weir and his artist friends called it, the mythical land of dreams. The landscape of stone walls, gently sloping pastures, orchards, and woodlands is rural

ANDI MARIE CANTELE

An artists' haven in rural Wilton

Connecticut at its most typically picturesque, and it inspired some of Weir's and his friends' best work.

Weir's innovative style left a high-water mark for every American impressionist to come in his wake, and as a founder of the prestigious group of artists known as the Ten American Painters (or "The Ten"), he helped nurture a new movement in American art. But early in his career, Weir followed in the footsteps of the Dutch masters—and his artist father—by painting portraits and still lifes, accurate renderings within the strictures of realism. That changed once he discovered the French impressionists and their sketchy style while studying at the École des Beaux-Arts in Paris. They painted outdoors, *en plein air*, rather than in a studio, to capture people and nature in candid moments.

So he purchased the farm, built a studio, and began painting beyond the portrait, turning instead to his surroundings. Unlike the sweeping Hudson River School landscapes popular in the day, Weir looked at the countryside with a personal eye, creating images of pastoral idyll at an intimate level.

"Home is the starting place," Weir once remarked, and thus painted simple images of pastures, barnyard animals, and ordinary domestic scenes, all in his trademark palette of soft blues, greens, and purples. His work bears the mark of the impressionists' fascination with nature and light, but it took a more personal stance—a farmer tilling the land, a child playing in the barnyard, or his wife, Ella, sewing near the pond.

With Jamie, our guide on the park's studio walking tour, we strolled the patchwork of meadows and deep woods, past undulating stone walls, the apple orchard, and the "secret garden."

"There's a snapshotlike, in-the-moment quality to many of his domestic scenes," she said, as we milled around the English-style post-and-beam barn. There, from a stack of prints, she pulled out one of his young daughter, playing in the very spot in which we were standing. In front of Weir's Greek-revival farmhouse, we looked at *Idle Hours,* showing his wife and daughter relaxing on a sofa while their dogs slept in front of the fireplace.

Later, continuing a long-held tradition among visiting artists, and doing her part to fulfill the park's mission of "reuniting art with the land-

IF YOU GO:

Weir Farm National Historic Site *(203-834-1896; www.nps.gov /wefa), 735 Nod Hill Rd., Wilton. Grounds are open daily from dawn to dusk; the Burlingham House Visitor Center is open May through October, Wednesday through Sunday 8:30–5; November through April, Thursday through Sunday 10:00–4; closed major holidays. Admission and tours are free; ask about studio and stone-wall walking tours, or pick up a brochure ($2) for the self-guided Weir Farm Historic Painting Sites Trail.* **Getting there:** *From I-84 follow US 7 south to the Branchville section of Ridgefield. Turn right onto CT 102, left onto Old Branchville Road, then left at first stop sign onto Nod Hill Road.*

scape that inspired it," Lisa set up her wooden easel in the terrace garden designed by Weir's daughter, Cora. I watched over her shoulder as she slid brand-new oil pastels from their box and began sketching with quick, sure strokes. By late afternoon the sun began slipping toward the horizon, the peonies, foxgloves, and fragrant boxwood were suffused with the same soft color and light reminiscent of Weir's paintings, and that's when the sensation hits me: I was looking at a picture within a picture, and the latest in a long line of artists to work in the footsteps of the masters.

Pick Your Own Fun

Lyman Orchards, Middlefield

As we head into the orchard, baskets in hand, we'd be hard-pressed to imagine a more perfect fall day: a cloudless October sky, dazzling foliage, and the promise of fresh-off-the-branch apples. And there they are, in all their crunchy, juicy abundance: Macouns. Honeycrisps. Galas. Ida Reds.

We're at Lyman Orchards in Middlefield—worth a trip from anywhere in the state—to pick fruit in the midst of some of Connecticut's prettiest countryside. Early varieties such as Empress and Ginger Gold start coming in around mid-August, but most of the state's apple picking begins in September, when McIntosh apples ripen. Our prospects look good: Local farmers say they're seeing fat apples in the orchard this year, thanks to high temperatures and plenty of rain.

Of all the pick-your-own establishments found in the state, many are farms for all seasons, where day-tripping visitors can take to the fields and orchards for strawberries in mid-June, veggies and blueberries in summer, bright-orange pumpkins and bushels of apples in fall, and Christmas trees in December. On September and October weekends, many shuttle pickers to the apple orchard or pumpkin patch via tractor- or horse-drawn hay wagon to enjoy the foliage and the fruit picking.

Take the Lyman family, whose farm is one of the last in a town once full of farms. John Lyman III is the eighth generation to work the land, a 1,100-acre spread in operation since 1741, when John and Hope Lyman purchased 36 acres back when Middlefield, like much of Connecticut, was

CORY MAZON

Pick-your-own farms welcome visitors from spring to fall.

virtually covered in farmland. "Pretty much the whole town was a farm back then," Lyman said, "with different families owning pieces of it."

The state is losing about 9,000 acres of its 300,000 acres of farmland every year, says the Connecticut Farmland Trust, a private organization that buys development rights from farmers. The farms that remain are, for the most part, small family-run ventures, and for 21st-century farmers hanging tough against encroaching suburbia and skyrocketing land values, success hinges on the ability to adapt and diversify. With forward thinking and a healthy dose of luck, many of the state's large-scale farms have shifted to specialty operations, from wineries and grass-fed beef to you-pick operations. It even has a name: "agratainment." The Lymans' farm is planted with some 40,000 peach, pear, and apple trees, and 20 acres of field crops like berries, pumpkins, and cut flowers. The rest? A pair of championship golf courses, built in the 1960s when the family phased out its dairy herd, plus a farm store, horse-drawn wagon rides, and lots of seasonal family events, from July's Blueberry Festival to autumn's 4-acre corn maze.

And, of course, produce ripe for the picking. Apple seeds and trees made their way to America early in the 17th century, and while more than 60 types of apples are grown in Connecticut, there are, according to the Connecticut Apple Marketing Board, some 7,500 varieties of apples in existence. The pick-your-own phenomenon began in the '60s as a way for small farmers to sell directly to consumers, who love the "farmer for a day" chance to head into the fields, to be sure. But the concept is evolving, Lyman says, into a delightfully old-fashioned, fun family outing, where parents go home with a greater appreciation and understanding of the rigors of living off the land, and youngsters see how fruit is grown and harvested before landing in the produce aisle.

"People like the idea of going out and rolling up their sleeves a bit," Lyman acknowledged, pointing to the loyal customers who come every week during the growing season. "But it's becoming more about the family getting together to spend a day at a farm in the country, and not just for picking."

IF YOU GO:

Lyman Orchards *(860-349-1793; crop hotline: 860-349-6015; www.lymanorchards.com), junction of CT 157 and CT 147, Middlefield.* **Getting there:** *Follow I-84 to I-691, which leads to US 66 east. In Middlefield turn right onto CT 147, then bear right onto CT 157.*

Think the growing season comes to an end with summer? Think again. In Connecticut, many crops peak when the air turns crisp. By autumn, fields are dotted with pumpkins and orchards are full of apples, but while those are the top crops to peak when the leaves change color, at some farms you can pick pears, plums, peaches, gourds—even late-season annuals and perennials. Click on www.pickyourown.org for a complete list of Connecticut farms offering pick-your-own produce and more, or contact the state Department of Agriculture (860-713-2503; www.ct.gov/doag/), which produces the "Connecticut Farm Map," a full-color state highway map featuring descriptive listings of pick-your-own farms, farm businesses, and farmers' markets. To request a free map, send a self-addressed, number 10 business-size envelope (or larger) with 87 cents worth of postage to the Connecticut Farm Map, Connecticut Department of Agriculture-Marketing, 165 Capitol Avenue, Room G-8A, Hartford, CT 06106. The department also publishes a variety of free brochures, including ones on apple growers and pick-your-own farms.

Fresh-from-the-orchard fruit holds flavor that can never be duplicated on supermarket shelves, the attendant told us as she weighed our apples and I bit into a deep-red Liberty with a snappy *crunch*. It was no surprise, of course, since anyone who has ever picked their own fruit will tell you the same thing. From the apples people cart home will no doubt come cakes, cobblers, and chunky, cinnamon-scented sauce, not to mention the crisp, crunchy fruit packed in lunches to be eaten out of hand. And if it's homemade pies you crave, just follow the aroma wafting from the Apple Barrel Farm Store, Connecticut's largest indoor farm market. For us, the choice is easy: the "hi-top" pie, a perennial winner in *Connecticut Magazine*'s Best of Connecticut apple pie category, made with farm-grown fruit filling a flaky golden crust and snapped up in an instant by folks who insist they're better than grandma's. Toting one pie and two baskets full of perfect crimson orbs, we agreed it was a perfect day of picking.

Sentimental Journey

The Naugatuck Valley Railroad and the Railroad Museum of New England

From our seats aboard a 1920s-era passenger train, the landscape suddenly looked foreign, as if we were in some strange new land instead of one of the most familiar places in the world. The winding Naugatuck River, the cliff-studded hills, and the dense stands of hemlock could have been a wilderness out the window. Instead, we were chugging through Mattatuck State Forest, a wooded oasis that literally surrounds our home, and whose trails we have explored too many times to count.

But today it all seemed so mysterious and wonderful and strange, a faraway country right in our own backyard. I flashed on *The Polar Express*, the children's tale where a magical train appears at a boy's doorstep on Christmas Eve to whisk him off to the North Pole.

We were, in fact, passengers aboard the Naugatuck Railroad, on one of the scenic excursions offered by the Railroad Museum of New England. And while the railroad long ago left town, its legacy can be traced along the river in Thomaston, where vintage cars rest in the rail yard, some awaiting restoration, others spiffed up and ready to roll. The museum proper is housed in the restored 1881 Thomaston Station, but most visitors come to take the ultimate sentimental journey, which is not for train buffs only. Anyone young or young at heart will love the mix of history, scenery, and mechanical marvels on the 20-mile nostalgic trip on "the Naugy."

Climbing aboard the train into passenger coach #4980, built in 1924 by the Canadian Car Foundry for Canadian National Railways, there's no mistaking that you're embarking on a nostalgic trip—a ticket taker with regulation uniform and cap punched our tickets as the train pulled away from the station and began its slow rumble south along the river, past the old mills and brass works that put the valley on the map in the 20th century. The spartan decor is a far cry from the original splendor of the coaches, which boasted gleaming mahogany woodwork, gaslights, velour seats, and carpeting. That's when the cars were built for comfy cross-country travel, long-distance routes across Canada from Toronto to the Pacific Ocean.

The original Naugatuck line opened in 1849 and ran from Bridgeport to Winsted; the last passenger train left Thomaston Station in 1958. Trains carried raw materials in and left with clocks, machinery, and brass products made in factories along the river, enabling the Seth Thomas Company to produce more of its famous clocks, and the Plume & Atwood factory to produce more brass lamps, now popular collectibles on eBay.

"It was immediately the most profitable railroad in the country," said Ralph Harris, president of the volunteer-run museum. Waterbury's main station, whose iconic brick clock tower can be seen rising over the city from I-84, served the second-busiest train yard in New England during World War II, when the clock industry made detonators for bombs, and the brass factories turned out shell casings and uniform buttons. Restoration of Thomaston Station is under way to restore it to its 1950s' glory. "They wanted something to impress people from out of town when they stepped off the train," Harris said.

Today, thousands of children drag their parents along for special excursions with Santa Claus, the Easter Bunny, and Thomas the Tank Engine. Adults love the fall foliage trips and the engineer-for-an-hour program that lets wannabes run the locomotive up and down the line.

At the Thomaston Dam, a U.S. Army Corps of Engineers project commissioned after the 1955 flood, the diesel-electric locomotive once used for running freight for the Providence & Worcester Railroad was put to

The Naugatuck Valley Railroad picks up passengers at historic Thomaston Station.

work, pulling us across the face of the dam for the best views of the morning: rolling green hills, tall pines, and rugged cliffs. Harris instructed us to watch for the deer, fox, beaver, and red-tailed hawks often seen near the tracks.

On the way back to the station, we were lulled by the clickety-clack of the rails and the landscape out the window rolling by like a silent film. We eavesdropped on the elderly couple sitting across the aisle as they exchanged memories of train trips taken long ago. As we pulled into the station at journey's end, we felt much farther away from home than a handful of miles, and we knew we would never hike our woods again without hoping to hear that lonely whistle breaking the silence.

IF YOU GO:

Railroad Museum of New England *(860-283-7245; www.rmne .org), off East Main St. (US 6), Thomaston. Train rides May through mid-October, Tuesday, Saturday, and Sunday, plus special themed excursions.* **Getting there:** *exit 20 off I-84 to CT 8 northbound; take exit 38, turn left off ramp, bear right at sixth light onto East Main Street, go two blocks to station; from CT 8 southbound take exit 40 and follow the signs to the museum.*

MORE RAILROADING

Essex Steam Train & Riverboat *(860-767-0103; 1-800-377-3987; www.essexsteamtrain.com), One Railroad Ave., Essex (exit 3 off CT 9). Open daily mid-June through August; Friday through Sunday May through mid-June and September; Wednesday through Sunday in October. The Connecticut Valley Line's coal-fired locomotives pull authentically restored vintage railroad cars to Deep River, where pas-sengers board the* Becky Thatcher, *a Mississippi-style riverboat, for a steam up the Connecticut River, returning to Essex on the rails. The* Essex Clipper, *Connecticut's only dinner train, offers white-linen din-ing aboard 1920s-era Pullman cars.*

Danbury Railway Museum *(203-778-8337; www.danbury.org /drm), 120 White St., Danbury, occupies the restored 1903 Union Station, a museum with running model-train displays and exhibits on railroad history, while passenger coaches, cabooses, steam locomotives, freight cars, and the only operating turntable in Connecticut fill a 6-acre rail yard; Saturday rail excursions from spring to fall.*

Connecticut Eastern Railroad Museum *(860-456-9999;*

www.cteastrrmuseum.org), 55 Bridge St./CT 32, Willimantic, features a restored Railroad Village with train equipment, a freight house, 19th-century station, telegrapher's shanty, and rides aboard an authentic pump car.

ALL EYES ON THE SKIES

Bird Watching on Long Island Sound

The sun rises at 7:03 on October 15 in Madison. I know this because I have just driven clear across the state, northwest quadrant to southern shoreline, waking at an ungodly hour to arrive at Hammonasset Beach State Park at sunup. Why? Birds. Lots and lots of birds. Southbound migrants, to be exact, which have been moving through this renowned birding hot spot in huge numbers lately.

Or so I'm told. Me, I'm no birder, but the thought of on-the-move songbirds, shorebirds, and raptors is enough to lure me here. It's migration time in Connecticut, and the birds are converging—tens of thousands of them, cruising along their annual routes and propelled by primal urges toward their winter quarters. Birders, too, feel the pull of the season. For pros, the autumn approach of hawks and warblers and cormorants means the time has come once again to polish up the scopes, dust off the field guides, and head to the shore. For neophytes, the guided migratory birding walks along the coast hosted by the Connecticut Audubon Society are a great introduction to the allure of casual bird watching. It's called avitourism, and some 70 million Americans are taking part.

So under a bright robin's-egg-blue sky, 20 of us took the path to Willard Island, led by Andy Griswold, director of Connecticut Audubon's EcoTravel program. With necks draped in optical gear, or toting spotting

The Connecticut coast is a mecca for birding.

scopes and tripods, we were experts and novices alike. With borrowed binoculars and a library copy of *Stokes Field Guide to Birds*, I fell solidly in the latter category. No matter, there were birds, birds, everywhere: in the woods, in the fields, in the marshes.

Connecticut's largest public beach park is all about sun, sand, and surf in summer, but when the lifeguards stop blowing their whistles and the suntanned masses are long gone, Hammonasset morphs into a birders' mecca. It's in the path of the Atlantic Flyway, a major bird migration route navigated by legions of feathered travelers who assemble on the coast as they wing their way through the state to their wintering grounds, some as far south as Argentina and Chile. Others that spend their summers up north might stay here and become part of Connecticut's winter bird population. The diverse habitats along the shore—meadow and salt marsh, freshwater and ocean—meet the needs of the migrants who come to rest, eat, and nest.

MORE BIRDING

Early birds will find that dawn over Long Island Sound is beautiful. The earlier you arrive, the better your chance for superb birding. After all, the early bird … well, you know the rest. Enjoy (and don't forget your bird books and binoculars)!

Barn Island Wildlife Management Area *(860-424-3000), Palmer Neck Rd., Stonington*

Bluff Point State Park *(860-444-7591), Depot Rd., Groton*

Connecticut Audubon Coastal Center *(203-878-7440), One Milford Point Rd., Milford*

Lighthouse Point Park *(203-946-8790), Two Lighthouse Rd., New Haven*

Sandy Point *(203-937-3651), Beach St., West Haven*

Sherwood Island State Park *(203-226-6983), Sherwood Island Connector, Westport*

Griswold showed us how to identify birds based on plumage, voice, behavior, and habitat. We got good looks at spotted eastern towhees, eastern phoebes, and vesper sparrows, and were delighted when he coaxed a ruby-crowned kinglet into the sunlight by imitating the call of an eastern screech owl. We watched day-to-day survival dramas play out, from a mockingbird chasing off a starling to northern harriers hunting the marshes in search of a meal. Others we only heard—the sputtery call of a Carolina wren, the sharp chip notes of a cardinal, and then, a new sound: the distinctive *tsee, tsee, tsee* call of a golden-crowned kinglet from somewhere in the cedars. The junipers and cherry trees looked like the perfect spot for birds to gather. And it was: A gray catbird landed on a branch above us and looked my way. True to its name, it gives a catlike *meow* call when alarmed, but when I edged a bit closer, it didn't flinch.

A visit to the Connecticut shore in October also brings the chance to glimpse osprey; we gasped in admiration as one of the magnificent, fish-eating birds of prey circled over our heads. Next I trained on a bird I hadn't heard of until recently—the greater yellowlegs—which at the moment was twittering in the salt marsh as it skimmed the shallows for snacks. To my untrained eye, the brown creeper looked pretty ordinary, but the experienced birders were delighted to see it. They were equally electrified by the sight of a rarely observed red-headed woodpecker. It didn't stay long, probably less than two minutes, but gave us an excellent peek at its black-and-white wing pattern and crimson head. We don't see a lot of them in Connecticut, Griswold noted, even though woodpeckers—downy, red-bellied, and hairy—are common. For me, the highlight of the morning was the ghostly figure of a great blue heron floating over a field. They nest in Connecticut, so this one could have been either a local resident or a migrant.

Nearly four hours of peering through binoculars and consulting bird-identification books paid off—we had been treated to what Griswold called "a nice laundry list of good birds," and I decided that birding is one of the most enjoyable, unheralded outdoor pleasures around. By November,

IF YOU GO:

Hammonassett Beach State Park *(203-245-2785; www.dep.state .ct.us/stateparks/parks/hammonasset.htm), 1288 Boston Post Rd. (US 1), Madison.* **Getting there:** *Exit 62 off I-95; follow the Hammonassett Connector to the park.* **Connecticut Audubon Society EcoTravel** *(1-800-996-8747; www.ctaudubon.org); check the Web site for a schedule of avian events and naturalist-guided bird walks.*

virtually every migrant heading for the tropics will clear out of New England, but I'm already pining for spring, when the yellow-rumped warblers, Cooper's hawks, and all their feathered ilk will pass through again. And while we had especially good luck with sparrows—about a dozen species turned up—the day yielded just one bluebird—flitting around in the sumacs—but the audience seemed satisfied. I would love to have seen it, but its bubbly song was worth the early morning trip.

SMALL STATE, BIG HIKE

The Appalachian Trail

From atop Bear Mountain, Connecticut's highest peak, the three-state view is none too hard on the eyes. Viewed from 2,316 feet, the pleasing palette of woods and farmers' fields punctuated by sparkling lakes and, beyond, the blue-hued Berkshires, is one of the most striking vistas anywhere in the state.

It was half an hour before sunset on an early September evening, cool and still bright, with a trace of the long, languorous summer left in the air. The heat, skeeters, and crowds had all moved on, but foliage hadn't yet tinged the landscape. We were wind-blown and trail-weary but cheerful. It was the last leg of a three-day sojourn on the granddaddy of America's long trails, the Appalachian National Scenic Trail, known among hikers simply as the AT.

The best part: We never left Connecticut.

Backpacking in Connecticut? You bet. While the thought doesn't exactly bring to mind pristine wilderness, the nation's oldest long-distance footpath offers a bit-of-everything sampler as it takes hikers through some of the most rugged and beautiful terrain in the state. In 2,175 miles, the AT links Springer Mountain in Georgia to Maine's Mount Katahdin, crossing 14 states, 8 national forests, and 6 national parks as it follows the spine of the Appalachians across all manner of jaw-dropping topography.

While short hikes fit nicely into most of our overscheduled lives, there's nothing like a few off-the-grid days to leave you wondering about priorities in today's busy, multitasking world. So three days earlier, Brian and I picked up the trail near the New York state line in Kent. The plan: Follow Connecticut's 52-mile segment north all the way to Massachusetts.

Think Connecticut's modest stretch won't challenge you? Think again. Sure, it's mellower than, say, what you'd find in the Smokies or Whites, but for a small state, it certainly packs in a variety of terrain. The trail rises quickly on short, steep climbs up slopes thick with trees and over ridgetops before crossing the state's highest peaks—Mount Riga, Lion's Head, Prospect Mountain, the aforementioned Bear Mountain—clustered in Connecticut's extreme northwest corner.

In the 1920s, forester Benton MacKaye envisioned a continuous trail connecting the highest peak in the South, North Carolina's 6,684-foot Mount Mitchell, with the highest peak in the Northeast, New Hampshire's 6,288-foot Mount Washington. The AT opened in 1937, and the entire route is marked with ubiquitous white blazes—165,000 in all—painted on trees, boulders, and posts.

Of the 4 million people on the trail every year, about 2,500 hardy souls attempt the entire Georgia-to-Maine shebang in one season. It's a tough slog, to be sure, and we were hoping to come across one of these long-haul hikers, known on the trail as through-hikers. Most leave Georgia in spring with the intention of reaching northern New England before the snow flies—a plan that puts them in Connecticut during the summer. Maybe we'd meet Crazy Legs, Rocket Shoes, or Path Pounder (it's a long-held tradition among through-hikers to adopt a trail name), names we heard had been seen scrawled in trail registers this season. Sure enough, on the second day we spotted a white-bearded hiker bent under a ponderous backpack plodding up Sharon Mountain. We remained duly impressed upon learning the 60-year-old retired science teacher was just "taking a walk across New England."

This being the 21st century, many through-hikers turn to trail registers in cyberspace. "I was very surprised by Connecticut," one wrote. "For such a short section, it is very diverse."

ROD JOHNSON

The Appalachian Trail cuts across Connecticut's northwest corner.

"It seems to have it all," another agreed, "from a stroll along a river-bank to the ruggedness of St. John's Ledges."

To be sure, we were surprised by how the trail tested our mettle. The old axiom—two steps forward, one step back—came to mind early on, but by the 20-mile mark we had found our rhythm, striding in perfect unison and making incredibly good time. On our last full day, we stopped at a sloping farm field for a moment of total silence (solitude is still the AT's top draw, even though you'll likely run into others, especially on weekends). As the afternoon edged into evening, we opted to pitch the tent instead of bunking in one of the trail's three-sided shelters. After dinner we lounged under a sky white with stars. There was a time when bagging the entire trail was on our dream itinerary, but the 5 million or so footsteps—about four to six months—required to complete the journey just doesn't fit into our reality, or dreams, these days. We crawled into the tent and slept fitfully until the sun crept up. At first light, we were bleary-eyed but ready to slip on our boots and load our gear on our backs for the last time. Abiding the Leave No Trace ethic, we collected all evidence of ourselves and eased out onto the trail.

On Bear Mountain, we pondered the landscape below us—at this height, we could see clear to the Catskills and Green Mountains—and recounted the trip's high points: the scramble down St. John's Ledges, the gentle amble along the Housatonic River, the plum vista from Rand's View. By now it was late afternoon, and the urgency to get off the trail before dark was as strong as the urge to keep going. But we paused at a critical junction: To the right, the Paradise Lane side trail led to our car; to the left, the AT's white blazes pointed the way 700 miles north to Mount Katahdin. We lingered as long as we could, grateful for the chance to step out of our high-octane day-to-day, then hoisted up our packs and walked back to civilization.

IF YOU GO:

For information on the trail, contact the **Appalachian Trail Conservancy** *(304-535-6331; www.appalachiantrail.org), P.O. Box 807, Harpers Ferry, WV 25425-0807, or the* **Appalachian Mountain Club** *(617-523-0655; www.outdoors.org), Five Joy St., Boston, MA 02108. The Connecticut chapter (www.ct-amc.org) organizes trail mainte-nance on the state's portion of the Appalachian Trail and its access trails.* **Getting there:** *You can step on the trail at US 41 in Salisbury, or one of its junctures with US 7, including Sharon, Kent, or farther south at Bulls Bridge in South Kent.*

CONNECTICUT'S QUIET CORNER

On and Along Route 169

Shhh!

Travel writers invariably invoke the term "sleepy" when describing the rural region tucked away in northeast Connecticut's Quiet Corner. It's been called many things. "An unsung nook" praised *National Geographic.* "Uninterrupted tranquility," gushed *Yankee.* It's also known as the Last Green Valley, a 1,085-square-mile swath whose official name is the Quinebaug and Shetucket Rivers Valley National Heritage Corridor. At half the size of Grand Canyon National Park, it's a big draw in a small state (part of the expanse stretches into Massachusetts), and with more than 70 percent of it covered in fields and forests, it's most certainly green. At night, from airplane or by satellite, it appears as a dark blotch in the Boston-to-Washington urban sprawl. From the ground, it's a bucolic landscape dotted with quiet villages offering old-time diversions—a taste of New England as it used to be.

Whatever you call it, it's as soothing a landscape as they come in the Northeast, an enclave where pockets of sleepy peacefulness seem newly acquainted with the twenty-first century. If the New England of your dreams includes charming bed and breakfasts and antiques shops, centuries-old villages surrounding proud town greens, farm stands heaped with pears and apples, plowed-up fields laced with crumbling stone walls, and few tourists, dream no more. In fact, it blends all this variety in such

Roseland Cottage is a pink icon along CT 169.

ROBERT GREGSON FOR CONNECTICUT CULTURE & TOURISM

a neat package that if I were to choose one destination to embody the spirit of rural Connecticut, the Quiet Corner would be it.

So we head north on CT 169, a lovely ribbon of blacktop whose old-fashioned scenery is perfect for slow-motion sightseeing. Spend a little time on this historic highway—one of only two Connecticut roads designated a national scenic byway—and it becomes clear how the Quiet Corner earned its quaint moniker. We started our explorations in Lisbon, a tiny 18th-century town where Heritage Trail Vineyards (860-376-0659; www.heritagetrail.com) offers French-American hybrids such as Quinebaug White and Shetucket Red, named for the region's major rivers. In Canterbury, the Prudence Crandall Museum (860-546-9916) is a handsome 1805 home complete with changing exhibits telling the story of racial tensions that stirred a rural Connecticut village decades before the Civil War. Briefly told: Crandall opened New England's first academy for black girls here in 1833. The problem? In Connecticut at the time, it was illegal to educate "young ladies and little misses of color," curator Kaz Kozlowski explained, so chaos ensued—a mob of locals vandalized the school, and Miss Crandall was all but run out of town. Eventually, Connecticut made amends—a century after her death, she was named the state's official heroine.

In Brooklyn, settled in the 1600s, Creamery Brook Bison (860-779-0837; www.creamerybrookbison.com) is a working farm where wagon rides take visitors to where buffalo roam, and a retail shop sells bison meat and fresh ice cream. Brooklyn Café and Antique Shoppe offers light homemade fare, antiques, and books in a hard-to-miss pink house, but many take a quick detour to the Golden Lamb Buttery, where guests enjoy a hayride around Hillandale Farm's thousand pastoral acres before dining on seasonal gourmet cuisine in the barn. Next time, we vow.

Further north in Pomfret, Lapsley Orchards (860-928-9186) is a 200-acre family farm where horse-drawn hayrides stop in the orchard for pick-your-own apples and pumpkins. For quiet woods and history, Mashamoquet Brook State Forest (860-928-6121) is legendary. Trails offer a long list of possibilities for the outward bound; we follow the arrows leading to the wolf den where, folklore says, Revolutionary War hero General Israel "Don't fire until you see the whites of their eyes" Putnam tracked and shot the last she-wolf in Connecticut. Nearby, the Vanilla Bean Café (860-928-1562; www.thevanillabeancafe.com), known around here simply as The Bean, is beloved not only for its award-winning chili and to-die-for desserts but for its tight weave into the fabric of the community. A loyal coterie of locals mingles with throngs of "gentlemen bikers" who make the trip from all over on weekends. We stayed for an evening of acoustic folk music, then spent the night at the Mansion at Bald Hill (860-974-3456; www.mansionatbaldhill.com), a grand South Woodstock estate-turned-homey-bed-and-breakfast. In the formal wood-paneled library, a soaring space boasting one the mansion's 13 fireplaces, I felt like Mrs. Bowen, the turn-of-the-20th-century railroad heiress who summered here.

We resisted the temptation to scrap the rest of our plans in favor of more mansion lounging. In the rural hilltop town of Woodstock (settled in 1686), Roseland Cottage (860-928-4074) presides in all its salmon-hued Gothic-revival splendor. Here, New York newspaper publisher Henry Bowen hosted four U.S. presidents (Hayes, Grant, Benjamin Harrison, and McKinley); today's visitors can admire the stained-glass windows, original furnishings, century-old boxwood parterre garden, and one of the oldest bowling alleys in the nation. And for a spot of tea any-time, Mrs. Bridge's Pantry (860-963-7040; www.mrsbridgespantry.com) is run by Veronica Harris and Diana Jackson, expatriate Englishwomen who serve crumpets, scones with clotted cream, and a traditional ploughman's lunch. They're also purveyors of all things tea—pots, infusers, cozies, and gifts from the British Isles.

Our 32-mile foray ends just shy of the Massachusetts border, so we take a quick side trip to "Central New England's Antiques Capital." Until the 1980s, Putnam was just another casualty of New England's postindustrial age, but its renaissance is a success story of the finest kind. The old brick mill town has recast itself as a mecca of all things antique, where dealers peddle relics from the past out of a dozen historic storefronts and rambling old cotton factories jammed with vintage goods of all kinds. Downtown, antiques literally spill onto the sidewalk; just pick your century and let the browsing begin. "Where do they get all this stuff?" you may ask

---

IF YOU GO:

Quinebaug-Shetucket Heritage Corridor, Inc. *(860-963-7226; 1-866-363-7226; www.nps.gov/qush) offers brochures on local attractions and events, including October's popular Walking Weekends series of more than a hundred free guided excursions.* **Getting there:** *The southern terminus of CT 169 is located just off I-395 (exit 81) in Norwich.*

---

yourself. We imagine possible uses for bride-and-groom wedding cake toppers, Limoges china, and a 1920s-era Victrola record player.

Putnam proved itself worth the detour, and we leave town empty-handed but full of inspiration. Back on CT 169, it's time to think about heading home. But before we do, we make one last stop, this time at the Connecticut Audubon Center at Pomfret (860-928-2939; www .ctaudubon.org). The 700-acre tableau of forests, streams, and meadows—and its top-notch birding—beckons for us to linger, but the sun is setting, and there's a pink hue in the sky. As night settles on the Quiet Corner, we roll down the windows and enjoy the silence, in all its quiet splendor.

Fruit of the Vine

The Connecticut Wine Trail

If you think life isn't complete without a little wine and cheese close at hand, and a whiff of buttery chardonnay sends your blood racing, then Connecticut's vineyards will make you very, very happy. They may not top the wine-tour circuit like, say, Napa, but the climate and soil are quite conducive to growing grapes and making wine. Thanks to 1978's Connecticut Winery Act, 16 commercial vineyards and wineries are in operation, a mix of family-run farm operations and small boutique wineries.

Sure, Connecticut's wine industry is small, compared with California's $45 billion behemoth. But local vintners are justly proud of their creations. And for oenophiles, and people who enjoy wine but haven't yet made a hobby of it, autumn is perfect for a ramble through the parts of the state given over to vineyards, some high in the hills, others near the shore.

Want to sound like an insider when you talk about wine? Tours offer a peek at the world of small-scale winemaking. At some you can even view art exhibits, enjoy live music in lovely settings, or learn how raspberries, blackberries, and other fresh-from-the-field fruits can, like grapes, become wine. The fruit of the Connecticut vine yields some nice surprises, and tastings will help you find your inner sommelier (or at least teach you to distinguish a sauvignon from a syrah).

Cheers!

Hopkins Vineyard on Lake Waramaug

HOPKINS VINEYARD, NEW PRESTON

After returning home from the Revolutionary War, Elijah Hopkins started working the land on the north shore of Lake Waramaug in 1787. Sheep, racehorses, and dairy cows have all been raised here, but in 1979 the family made the switch to grapes.

In the same spirit of new uses for old places, the 19th-century barn was converted into a winery, complete with tasting room, gift shop, and hayloft wine bar. Bill Hopkins, whose 30-acre vineyard bears his name, presides over grapes as lovely as the spot in the rolling Litchfield Hills. This is Connecticut's only vineyard, in fact, on an inland lake, which means a longer growing season and a microclimate that's well suited to cultivating several varieties of grapes, including chardonnay, pinot noir, and cabernet franc.

"The south-facing slopes facing the lake moderate the temperature and provide good breezes," Hopkins explained. "It's important for the vines to dry out in the morning."

Back in the winery, we sampled an '04 Westwind, a semisweet wine, and an estate-grown cabernet franc—not a bad bet. In the end, we're sold on the whimsically named Red Barn Red and Sachem's Picnic, and leave with a bottle of each.

IF YOU GO:

Hopkins Vineyard *(860-868-7954; www.hopkinsvineyard.com), 25 Hopkins Rd., New Preston. Open daily for tastings; reduced hours in winter and early spring. Guided group tours are by reservation only.* **Getting there:** *Take US 202 to CT 45; turn left onto Lake Road, then right onto Hopkins Road.*

SHARPE HILL VINEYARD, POMFRET

Connecticut's so-called Quiet Corner is a perfect stage for the Vollweiler family's 15-acre vineyard, whose orderly rows of vines are perched on a 700-foot slope surrounded by 100 idyllic acres and vistas stretching out toward Rhode Island and Massachusetts. Winemaker Harold Bursen transforms cabernet franc and chardonnay grapes into homegrown vintages, such as St. Croix and Riesling (both priced at about $18). The specialty: the award-winning Ballet of Angels, a semidry white packaged with a label bearing a historical painting of a boy holding a bluebird.

The winery is in an 18th-century-inspired building whose antiques-filled tasting room is reminiscent of a period taproom. The French-accented gourmet lunch in the Fireside Tavern or outdoors in the wine garden overlooking the vineyard is a special treat.

🪶 🪶 🪶 🪶 🪶 🪶 🪶 🪶

IF YOU GO:

Sharpe Hill Vineyard *(860-974-3549; www.sharpehill.com), 108 Wade Rd., Pomfret. The winery is open for lunch (reservations are essential) and tastings Friday through Sunday 11–5. Tours on request.* **Getting there:** *From US 44 turn south onto CT 97, then left onto Kimball Hill Road; the vineyard is 1.8 miles down the road.*

🪶 🪶 🪶 🪶 🪶 🪶 🪶 🪶

CHAMARD VINEYARDS, CLINTON

On a cool morning in early October, we took the back way to the shore to this coastal winery known for its chardonnays. The turning grape leaves were a riot of color—ocher, gold, crimson, and rust, with a touch of leftover green—and the mist hanging over the 20-acre vineyard was like a portal to the northern Italian countryside—Piedmont, to be exact, in the hills of Le Langhe.

Tiffany & Company exec William Chaney established his chateau-style winery on Cow Hill Road in 1983 (the operation changed hands in 2005). The vines are close to Long Island Sound, which means a choice microclimate of mild temperatures, rich soil, and a long growing season. Chamard produces 6,000 cases—that's 13,000 gallons—every year. Most are chardonnay, with some merlot, cabernet franc, cabernet sauvignon, and pinot noir tossed into the mix.

🪶 🪶 🪶 🪶 🪶 🪶 🪶 🪶

IF YOU GO:

Chamard Vineyards *(860-664-0299; www.chamard.com), 115 Cow Hill Rd., Clinton. Free tours and tastings Tuesday through Sunday 11–5.* **Getting there:** *Take exit 63 off I-95; follow CT 81 north, then turn left onto Cow Hill Road.*

🪶 🪶 🪶 🪶 🪶 🪶 🪶 🪶

Under the guidance of David, our young sommelier, Lisa and I tasted our way through the winery's premium line of handcrafted varietals, starting with their claim to wine fame, the straw-colored Estate Reserve Chardonnay, boasting 100 percent Chamard grapes. He instructed us on what to look for: buttery notes in the chardonnays, hints of blackberry and chocolate in the cabernet and merlot.

The informative—and free—tours give visitors a peek into the cellar, where state-of-the-art stainless steel vats share space with French oak barrels. We left this lovely place with a lesson on the finer points of winemaking and, naturally, a couple bottles of good libations.

MORE CONNECTICUT VINEYARDS

For information on the Connecticut Wine Trail, or to order a free brochure, call 860-267-1399, or click on www.ctwine.com.

Bishop's Orchards Winery *(203-453-2338; www.bishops orchardswinery.com), 1355 Boston Post Rd. (US 1), Guilford*

DiGrazia Vineyards *(203-775-1616; www.digrazia.com), 131 Tower Rd., Brookfield*

Gouveia Vineyards *(203-265-5526), 1339 Whirlwind Hill Rd., Wallingford*

Haight Vineyard *(860-567-4045; www.haightvineyards.com), 29 Chestnut Hill Road, Litchfield*

Heritage Trail Vineyards *(860-376-0659; www.heritagetrail .com), 291 North Burnham Highway, Lisbon*

Jerram Winery *(860-379-8749; www.jerramwinery.com), 535 Town Hill Rd., New Hartford*

Jonathan Edwards Winery *(860-535-0202; www.jedwards winery.com), 76 Chester Maine Rd., Stonington*

Jones Winery *(203-929-8425; www.jonesfamilyfarms.com), 266 Israel Hill Rd., Shelton*

Land of Nod Winery *(860-824-5225), 99 Lower Rd., East Canaan*

McLaughlin Vineyards *(203-426-1533; www.mclaughlin vineyards.com), Albert's Hill Rd., Sandy Hook*

Priam Vineyards *(860-267-8520), 11 Shailor Hill Rd., Colchester*

Stonington Vineyards *(860-535-1222; www.stonington vineyards.com), 523 Taugwonk Rd., Stonington*

White Silo Farm & Winery *(860-355-0271; www.whitesilo winery.com), 32 CT 37, Sherman*

Be A-Maze-d

The Corn Maze at White Hollow Farm, Lime Rock

"I think we're lost."

I had started suspecting as much. We were deep inside a larger-than-life 3-D puzzle carved into a cornfield way up in northwestern Connecticut, and our purposeful striding had downshifted into aimless wandering.

How hard could a corn maze be, we reasoned. Not only had we been dutifully following a map, but being the locals that we were, we had the advantage of familiar landmarks: the lump of Barrack Mountain rising above the Housatonic River to the east, the drone of race cars speeding around the track at Lime Rock Park just to the west.

We weren't quite hopelessly lost in the 11-acre cornfield at White Hollow Farm, but for a few moments we sure were stumped. No matter, it was a perfect day for losing oneself, one of those bright and warm September mornings in New England that fall fanatics dream about. Feathery tassels waved above our heads from atop 8-foot-tall cornstalks; beyond them, white puffs of cumulus clouds drifted slowly through a cobalt sky. A come-and-go breeze rustled the drying stalks and rushed down the corn rows forming living walls as far as the eye could see. Besides, I pointed out, not all those who wander, as J. R. R. Tolkien wrote, are lost. Brian barely glanced up from the map as I also pointed out the

Allen Cockerline

A maze of cornfields at White Hollow Farm

fiery orange wings of a monarch butterfly flitting overhead, or how the green hills ringing the cornfield hadn't yet taken on their spectacular red and gold finery.

Allen Cockerline had done his work well, and we told him so once we found our way back to the barn. It's no surprise: The longtime farmer has spent the past several years as one of the keepers—known as maze masters—of the designed fields of maize that are a growing autumn trend. These cunningly carved cornfields have become popular attractions around the country for families seeking fresh-air fun.

As Cockerline tells it, he needed something to do when he stopped milking cows, and like so many others exploring new ways to make a living off the land, the Litchfield County dairy farmer cut a field of corn into a maze. Many are professionally designed (think global positioning

---

MORE CONNECTICUT
CORN MAZES

Larson's Farm *(203-740-2790; www.larsonsfarm.com), 401 Federal Rd. (CT 133), Brookfield*

Lyman Orchards Corn Maze *(860-349-1793; www.lyman orchards.com), at the junction of CT 147 and CT 157, Middlefield*

Plasko's Farm *(203-268-2716; www.plaskosfarm.com), 670 Daniel's Farm Rd., Trumbull*

Merrow Corn Maze *(860-805-3276; www.merrowmaze.com), Merrow Rd., off CT 32, Storrs*

Preston Farms Corn Maze *(860-886-6293; www.prestonfarms cornmaze.com), 92 CT 2, Preston*

---

systems and high-tech computer gridding) and commercialized—NASCAR, Disney characters, Halloween, and patriotism are popular themes—but Cockerline is old school. After spending the winter designing the maze, he sets out with a tractor and six-row planter in May, dropping more than 300,000 corn seeds 2 inches deep in the field's loamy soil. When the young plants are a couple inches tall, usually around July 1st, he begins the ongoing process of removing rows to form paths and intersections to create the maze's geometric patterns. In early August, a local pilot flies him above the field to survey his work, and after he does some final edits back on the ground, visitors get to have a go at his creation: a living labyrinth with twists, turns, dead ends, and detours.

"We keep it intentionally impossible so you really get lost," Cockerline said. "For a lot of people, it's a real 'wow.'"

His simple-yet-effective design strategy is this: Start at impossible and work backward from there. And while the maze changes every year, it's always about what's going on in the fields. So our mission was not only to find our way through the maze, but to locate and identify the hidden crops growing within it, and answer a list of farming-themed trivia questions. The first inner field we stumbled upon sheltered mere remnants of a soybean crop wiped out by hungry deer and rabbits. Soon we found the Sudan grass grown for cattle feed; after that, winter rye, a popular cover crop on New England farms, then the cheery yellow heads of sunflowers nodding in the breeze. When we reached the circular clearing filled with white zinnias, one blossom was covered by the slowly beating wings of a monarch—resting, we figured, for its long journey south to Mexico.

By late October as many as four thousand visitors will have navigated the maze, and when they meet Cockerline, questions invariably revolve around farming. "People like to talk to a farmer," he noted (he and his wife, Robin, also run Whippoorwill Farm, a grass-fed beef business just down the road).

In the end, it took about an hour of maze meandering for us to complete the odyssey. For some, it's a chance to lose themselves; for others, a challenge to test their sense of direction amid the cornstalks. And for those who get too turned around, signs indicate the path that traces the field's perimeter.

IF YOU GO:

The **Corn Maze at White Hollow Farm** *(860-435-2089, 860-248-0362; www.cornmazect.com), at the junction of CT 112 and US 7, in the Lime Rock section of Salisbury, is open every Saturday and Sunday, as well as Monday holidays, from mid-August through October, 10–6; select Friday nights 7–10.* **Getting there:** *From I-84 take exit 7 and follow US 7 north to Salisbury; from Hartford take exit 39 off I-84 and follow CT 4 to US 7.*

"I tell people to lose themselves, just get lost," Cockerline said. "It's 11 acres. How lost can you really get?"

Quite, if you subscribe to the wisdom of trivia question number nine: When you come to a fork in the road, as Yogi Berra famously suggested, take it.

A Bonny Bash

The Scotland Highland Festival

I like to blend in when I travel. Unfortunately, due to wardrobe limitations, I had to attend the Scotland Highland Festival sans kilt, so I joined the thick crowd of spectators gathered at the historic Edward Waldo Homestead. Fittingly, this Highland festival is held in Scotland, a rural eastern Connecticut town named for the homeland of its first settler, and I timed my arrival to coincide with the opening ceremonies. It was an arresting sight: a colorful sea of tartan in electric yellow, crisp black and crimson, and cool blues and greens worn by bands, clans, and contestants—pipers, drummers, dancers, and athletes—parading across the festival grounds under a brilliant October sky.

There's no better place to channel your inner Scot than a Highland festival, a high-spirited celebration of all things Scottish, from kilts and cabers to sheepdogs and shortbread. Americans with Mac in their surnames keep alive the traditions that colonial immigrants brought from Scotland's fabled high country, the land of deep blue lochs and timeless turreted castles, whose traditional dress includes the kilts and tartans so widely associated with Scottish culture.

There's more to Scotland, of course, than bagpipes, kilts, and Loch Ness lore. Enter Highland festivals, whose nonstop revelry celebrates the heritage, culture, and traditions of the people known as Highland Scots. A maze of tents marks the gathering place for dozens of clans and Celtic

Highland cattle are easy to spot at the Scotland Highland Festival.

(people of Scottish, Irish, and Welsh descent) societies, from the Campbells and Maxwells to the Sutherlands and Fergussons. Nourishment comes by way of authentic food (hot meat pies) and grog (white birch beer). The sweet soda is a favorite quaff among festival-goers, who hunker down over fish-and-chips and mysterious ethnic curiosities with names like bridies, rumblethump, and bubble and squeak. Then there's haggis, the national dish traditionally made from a sheep's "pluck" (lungs, liver, and heart) boiled in a stomach. Here, according to a hand-written sign, it consisted of beef, liver, and onions tucked into a puff pastry. Nearby were purveyors of Scottish food and wares, from wool tartans fashioned into tams, sashes, ties, and, naturally, kilts, to digestives (cookies), spotted dick (steamed pudding), and other grocery items rarely found outside the United Kingdom. Crafts ran the gamut from drawings of thistle, Scotland's national flower, to sculptures of the legendary sea serpent of Loch Ness. "Nessie" is beloved among lads, lassies, and wee bairns, whose grandparents tell the tale of a murderous plesiosaur tamed by a sixth-century Irish monk. True or not, a full-blown tourist industry revolves around the creature inextricably linked to the deep freshwater lake in northern Scotland.

Most Highland gatherings revolve around competition, and here was no exception. Young girls in traditional dress charmed and captivated the audience as they spun and whirled in the balletlike Scottish lilt, the Highland fling, and the *ghillie chalium* (sword dance) once performed on the eve of battle. Highland athletics, my Scottish friends tell me, are also known as "heavy events," feats of strength and endurance deeply rooted in history and tradition. Athletes donned kilts to toss the hammer, the caber, and the sheaf to the delight of onlookers, who debated the origin of the games. While some opted for the idea that Scotland's chiefs and monarchs—the first games are often credited to Malcolm Canmore, an 11th-century Scottish king—needed a means to recruit soldiers and choose fast runners to serve as couriers, others clung to the notion that they began as funeral games honoring the mother of Lugh, the Celtic god of light.

MORE SCOTTISH EVENTS IN CONNECTICUT

Pipes in the Valley Celtic Music Festival *(860-870-5567; www.pipesinthevalley.com), Riverfront Plaza, Hartford*

St. Andrew's Society of Connecticut's Scottish Festival *(860-651-9048; www.sasct.org), Goshen Fairgrounds, CT 63, Goshen*

Round Hill Highland Games *(www.roundhill.org), Cranbury Park, Norwalk*

A rollicking Celtic band wowed the crowd with rousing harmonies, heartfelt ballads, ancient Gaelic melodies, and traditional Scottish dance tunes; elsewhere, music flowed from drums (*bodhrans*), flutes (*feadans*), harps (*clarsachs*), and, of course, bagpipes, an ancient instrument dating to 1500 B.C. Their haunting sound was everywhere, it seemed, drifting above the clan village and clear across the athletic field to the pastures where shaggy Highland cattle grazed and a young border collie named Flossie demonstrated the centuries-old sheepherding techniques used by farmers in Scotland's border hills. Responding to her trainer's voice commands and shrill whistles, she hustled a small flock of bewildered Katahdin sheep in various directions. Sometimes the sheep resist, "but if the dog is any kind of dog," Flossie's owner noted, "they don't do it for long."

You say Scotland and most people, of course, think kilts. The tailored, pleated tartan or tweed garment is the most recognized cultural tradition of the Highland Scots, but its origin is unknown to most people. Legend has it that the kilt, or *philabeg*, can be traced to early 10th-century Scottish and Irish clans; indeed, the multicolored arrangement of stripes and checks is paramount to a clan's identity. My untrained eye couldn't tell whether the elderly man in full Highland regalia was a MacDonald, MacDougall, or MacDuff, but his quiet, moving tribute to Scotland's beloved poet laureate Robert Burns, unnoticed by much of the passing crowd, was the highlight of the festivities:

> My heart's in the Highlands, my heart is not here;
> My heart's in the Highlands a-chasing the deer;
> A-chasing the wild deer, and following the roe—
> My heart's in the Highlands wherever I go.

IF YOU GO:

Scotland Highland Festival *(www.scotlandgames.org)*,
Edward Waldo Homestead, Waldo Rd., Scotland. **Getting there:**
From CT 14 in the center of Scotland, head south on CT 97 to the festival grounds.

Views You Can Use

Fall Foliage

The time between summer's unyielding temperatures and winter's flying snow—autumn, as we call it—is lovely for leaves. Heat and humidity have loosened their oppressive grasp, bringing a sigh of relief and waves of leaf peepers that descend on Connecticut with a madness for fall color that borders on fetish. But who can blame them? When the forest drops its leaves, hickories, maples, and birch turn honey, copper, and gold, painting a pretty picture in the hills.

The cusp-of-autumn show is not to be missed. What you'll want to miss are the crowds and tour buses that seem unavoidable on the road. To enjoy the scenery sans the tourists, lace up your boots and strike up any trail into the higher parts. At this colorful time of year, especially on weekends, some footpaths become veritable superhighways, as foliage fanatics happily tramp through the woods on invigorating hikes and easygoing rambles in search of Mother Nature's jewel-toned finery. But time it right and you'll be rewarded with paths you don't have to share, precious few humans in view, and the kind of silence that today's world seldom offers.

Don't wait—the annual autumnal extravaganza happens fast, and then is gone.

Heublein Tower, Talcott Mountain State Park, Simsbury

More at ease in the not-so-wild woods? You won't be alone as you trek

FOLIAGE FACTS

In Connecticut, the show usually peaks around Columbus Day weekend; the state **Department of Environmental Protection** *(www.dep.state.ct.us/updates/foliage) provides up-to-the-minute foliage reports in season. The* **Connecticut Forest & Park Association** *(860-346-2372; www.ctwoodlands.org), formed in 1895, maintains more than 800 miles of blue-blazed hiking trails perfect for viewing fall color.*

THE COLORS OF FALL

Yellow: ash, birch, silver maple, Norway maple, hickory
Bronze: beech, sugar maple, scarlet oak
Orange: sassafras, sumac
Red: ash, dogwood, red maple, oak
Purple: ash, dogwood, sassafras, sumac
Brown: silver maple

to one of Connecticut's iconic observation towers. If climbing the 120 steps up the Bavarian-style structure doesn't take your breath away, the view from the top surely will. The light-filled observation room boasts one of the state's best vistas: a 360-degree panorama across the Farmington River Valley, north to the Berkshires, and south to Long Island Sound.

The Heublein family's 1914 summer retreat atop Talcott Mountain is Connecticut's undisputed champion for attracting crowds: Some 130,000 visitors climb the tower every season. "There's no better place in Connecticut to see fall foliage," Kathryn Hoidge, president of Friends of Heublein Tower, tells me. "We've had people from 26 countries find their way here."

The 1.25-mile Tower Trail offers a quick woodland getaway that's perfect for a family outing; you can even take Fido along; just don't forget his leash. And if you don't like crowds, here's a tip: Visit during the week when the stream of leaf peepers turns into a trickle.

A vista in Kent

IF YOU GO:

Heublein Tower *(860-667-0662; www.friendsofheubleintower.org),
Talcott Mountain State Park, CT 185, Simsbury. Tower open Memorial
Day weekend to Labor Day, Thursday through Sunday 10–5; from
Labor Day to the last weekend in October, daily 10–5.*

COBBLE MOUNTAIN, MACEDONIA BROOK STATE PARK, KENT

I must admit, I'm so accustomed to this magnificent landscape of
ours in northwest Connecticut that I have to be reminded sometimes to
slow down and marvel at it. The busloads of tourists rumbling through in
fall inspire me to look around with a first-timer's fresh eyes.

To enjoy the color without the crowds, we head to Macedonia Brook
State Park in Kent and climb up Cobble Mountain for one of our all-time
favorite hikes. We love the vigorous clamber over the rocky scrambles and
steep sections, and no matter how many times we reach the lofty spot
that's more rocky outcropping than summit, we're amazed anew at the
pretty sweep of earth that opens before us—the rectangular farm fields
bare of trees, meadows demarcated by stone walls, and the rugged Taconic
and Catskill ranges (bring binoculars—you're likely to spy Cooper's hawks
and turkey vultures circling overhead).

A couple centuries ago, it is said, you could stand on a hilltop in
Litchfield County and see clear to Long Island Sound. That was during
the 18th and 19th centuries, when Connecticut was stripped bare of trees
by farmers, lumberjacks, and charcoal makers. Today's views are less
expansive but surely as lovely. We contemplate the russet-tinged trees and
the bright blue October sky, reluctant to leave save for what awaits us back
in town. Kent's Main Street is a perfect stop for the trailweary. Hungry
hikers go to Stroble Baking Company for sandwiches and to the Panini
Café for made-from-scratch gelato.

🖋 🖋 🖋 🖋 🖋 🖋 🖋 🖋

IF YOU GO:

Macedonia Brook State Park *(860-927-3238), 159 Macedonia Brook Rd., off CT 341, Kent. The park is open daily from 8 AM until dusk.* **Getting there:** *Take US 7 to Kent; follow CT 341 west for about 2 miles, then take the first right onto Macedonia Brook Road and follow it into the park.*

🖋 🖋 🖋 🖋 🖋 🖋 🖋 🖋

MOUNT MISERY, PACHAUG STATE FOREST, VOLUNTOWN

Looking out over rural eastern Connecticut from a rocky ledge atop Mount Misery, I was struck with a single thought: What's so miserable about this? Surely not the gentle ramble to the summit, just 441 feet above sea level. Definitely not the view, a tapestry of crimson and gold stretching into nearby Rhode Island.

This is *the* place in eastern Connecticut for foliage viewing, although the not-so-high ridgetop is a lovely place to be any time of year. We made quick work of reaching the modest summit, where raptors wheel in the sky in front of us and oaks, hickories, and maples glow in an electrifying blaze of color.

Pachaug State Forest is the largest of all Connecticut's forests, covering more than 24,000 acres along the Rhode Island border. Its 39 miles of woods roads and hiking trails promise a deep-in-the-woods adventure; it's also a good place to look at leaves with kids or older folks.

As magnificent as fall is, June boasts a not-to-be-missed sight: the profusion of pink and white blossoms as the forest's rhododendron sanctuary erupts in full bloom.

IF YOU GO:

Pachaug State Forest *(860-376-4075), CT 49, Voluntown. Open 8 AM to sunset.* **Getting there:** *From the center of Voluntown take CT 49 north to the forest entrance. Follow the forest road for 2 miles and bear left at the fork to reach the parking area. The woods access road on the left leads to the Mount Misery overlook.*

READY ALL, ROW
Connecticut's Fall Regattas

Sometimes even Joe Ryan realizes how crazy it is, this obsession of his.

"It's insane, really," said the Stamford executive with the telltale lean frame of a lifelong sculler. "I mean, I'm 61 years old. A 61-year-old shouldn't be doing this, right?"

Others in Connecticut who share the obsession with rowing tend to describe it in nearly the same terms. So it is that we fit into our lives dozens, if not hundreds, of sessions on the water each year, taking to lakes and rivers all over the state in the predawn darkness. For rowers, autumn is head race season, a last hurrah before racing wraps up and shuts down and our beloved waters freeze over, sending us indoors until spring.

Connecticut hosts three major regattas every October: the Head of the Riverfront and Head of the Connecticut on the Connecticut River, and the Head of the Housatonic on the Housatonic River. While short sprint races that match boats head to head make up the spring season, fall racing is all about endurance. In these "head of the river" events, similar in tradition to races held in England, rowers are let on a 3-mile-long course one at a time, time-trial style, to race against the clock. For athletes from around the country, Connecticut's regattas are tune-ups for the granddaddy of them all, the Head of the Charles, which draws thousands of crews to Boston's Charles River for the largest two-day rowing event in the world.

JERRY HYRES

The Head of the Housatonic Regatta in Shelton

New England's longest river flows through Connecticut's capital city on its journey to Long Island Sound, and on a steely-gray Sunday morning, Hartford's Head of the Riverfront regatta was a lively scene of rowers launching hundreds of sleek shells—singles, doubles, fours, and eights—dotting the water like confetti. They're all here: Resolutes and Fillipis, Van Deusens and Vespolis, crewed by high school teams, community rowing clubs, and hard-driven collegiate rowers dreaming of a seat on the U.S. national squad.

For rowers used to solitude and the low-angled light of sunrise, it's an exhilarating sight. Spectators need only claim a patch of riverbank (don't forget the binoculars), then relax and take in the crowd of cheering crew parents and rowing enthusiasts, and the passing parade of boats gliding up and down the river with a consummate grace that belies the grueling nature of the sport. Connecticut's tradition of rowing goes a long way back. All the way, in fact, to 1843, when Yale College formed the first collegiate boat club in the country, and 1878, when it began hosting

America's first collegiate sporting event—the Yale-Harvard regatta—on the Thames River in New London. Rowing enjoyed its golden days in the late 19th century, when the sport of oars gained a place in the popular imagination as a pursuit for the well-born few. Today, its ranks are filled with a blend of the elite and everyman, many of them folks taking up rowing later in life.

In our slender white-hulled shell, called the Tennessee, it was an easy paddle downstream to warm up before being called to the starting buoy. There, our crew of four masters (ages 27 and over) women executed a deft 180-degree pirouette as our coxswain navigated a tangle of roughly $500,000 worth of boats awaiting their turn to enter the chute of orange buoys funneling crews toward the start in 10-second intervals. When a race official nodded gravely at us and said "Litchfield, row!" we sprinted for 30 strokes before settling into a pace we could sustain for about 20 minutes. A stroke goes something like this: Rowers inch forward (the slide), bodies compressing like coiled springs, then plunk oar blades in the water (the catch) and push the boat forward with the legs (the drive), a pattern of motion repeated 600 or so times to reach the finish line in a typical head race.

There are races that begin well, and there are races that begin even better, but this one opened with a cold rain combined with a brisk wind to make conditions about as dicey as they get on a river. This was a different Connecticut from the one we saw last year, when sun shimmered off the water and foliage-clad hills glowed in the distance. Today, with waves coming over the port gunwale, we strained to move the Tennessee upriver. Winds and strong currents are not shy about swamping boats, so our coxswain steered us toward shore to find calmer water and maybe a break from the gusts kicking up. When we passed the cheering crowds at the Charter Oak Bridge and glided past Hartford's skyscrapers, he called for a Power 10, and we answered with a set of the most powerful strokes we could muster, leaving swirling puddles as we sprinted for the finish buoy.

Rowing is an up-before-dawn sport, but it has a mystical hold on most of us, which is perhaps why we wake up for 5:30 AM across-the-lake practice sessions and the endless drills that hone technique and build endurance. It's absurd, Ryan said, this notion of making rowing your life. Like me, he began as an eights rower at Boston University; now he's aiming for a masters title at the Head of the Charles, the holy grail of rowing.

"I've turned down opportunities at work because of rowing," Ryan admitted, as he prepped his single scull, a tippy 27-foot Empacher about a foot wide, for the men's masters race. Why? He would have missed too many sessions on the water.

"There's no better feeling in the world," he said. "I *have* to row."

IF YOU GO:

Head of the Riverfront *(www.riverfront.org), Charter Oak Landing, Hartford.* **Getting there:** *exit 27 off I-91.*

Head of the Housatonic *(www.newhavenrowingclub.org/ regattas), Indian Well State Park, CT 110, Shelton.* **Getting there:** *exit 14 off CT 8.*

Head of the Connecticut *(www.hctr.org), Harbor Park, Middletown.* **Getting there:** *exit 14 off CT 9.*

Artists' (New) Haven

City-Wide Open Studios

It began, like many good ideas do, over coffee. Helen Kauder and two friends were in San Francisco for an open studios tour, which, as its name implies, allows the cultured and the curious a peek at the work spaces of artists. "Wouldn't it be great if New Haven had something like this?" they mused afterward. Being the visionary art lovers that they are, they created one for their city. To their delight, two hundred artists showed up for what would in time become one of the premier cultural events in a city known for its culture.

The ambitious endeavor is known as City-Wide Open Studios, and since 1997 it has evolved from a weekend event to a 20-day "celebration of contemporary art" organized by Artspace, an artist- and volunteer-run nonprofit of which Kauder is the executive director. The October event— now the largest open studios festival on the East Coast— brings some five hundred artists together at locations around the city, from vast studio complexes and individual studios to an alternative-space venue that brings in artists from all over Connecticut.

Fascinated by New Haven's rep as the state's culture capital, I set out to meet some of these artists splashing paint around in studios in the Elm City. New Haven defies the stereotype of quaint old Connecticut, blending a European-style sophistication with a booming art scene. Historically a city of academe (Yale) and culture (museums, theaters, galleries), it's

LESLIE KUO FOR ARTSPACE

New Haven's artists open their doors every October.

ideally suited to a studio tour, and Erector Square is the ideal venue. The old A. C. Gilbert toy factory, where Erector Sets were once made, has been carved into studios, a labyrinthine brick complex where nearly 90 artists rent space and make up a diverse and vibrant community whose combined talent rivals any similar community in New York. I wandered in and out of studios where the work of sculptors, painters, photographers, craftspeople, and other artists covered the walls and floors. Studios run the gamut from comfortably cluttered to clean and ascetic, and showcase a range of approaches to painting. In one, bold Warhol-inspired self-portraits; in another, realistic American landscapes dramatically displayed to marvelous effect in a whitewashed room facing north, the preferred exposure for artists. Down the hall, exquisite art glass panels crafted of fossils, minerals, and metals cast an Old-World glow. In still another, a first-time tour participant brings an artist's eye to jewelry, specifically, polymer clay beads painted in whimsical patterns and hues strung together as earrings and necklaces. At the other end of the spectrum, a sculptor uses materials like paint cans and other industrial containers to transform discarded and forgotten items into new works, which bring with them a sense of reincarnation. There are drawings and digital images, too—including dreamy black-and-white snapshots and over-the-top murals that incorporate social commentary or that reference politics with a wink. Time will tell if there's a masterpiece among them.

Local work is shown in a more intimate setting in the self-guided tour of 30 working individual studios in attics, basements, even kitchens, in neighborhoods in and around the city. Rounding out the festival is the alternative-space event, which features vacant historic buildings used as temporary exhibition galleries. "Part of the fun for the audience is to see how the artists transform the space," Kauder explained. This year, it's an empty middle school—the nurse's office, the band rehearsal room, classrooms, locker rooms, even the kitchen's walk-in freezer are spaces for installations, giving artists from all over Connecticut, and locals without studio space, a coveted spot to work.

The tour is in line with Artspace's mission to "connect artists and audiences and redefine art spaces." For audiences, Kauder noted, it's a good time to see art being made and to purchase a painting, sculpture, or drawing directly from its maker without the gallery markup. For artists, it's a chance to share insights into how their art is created, talk about what inspires and motivates them, maybe even find the inspiration to get their portfolios together. And then there's that all-important exposure. Curators, dealers, gallery owners, and collectors come to discover new artists and buy never-before-seen works. It's also a rare chance to get out and visit other studios, see old artist friends, and meet some of the city's newest artists, "the kind of opportunities they don't have in the course of a normal day in the studio," Kauder said.

Artists are a lot like writers, I realized—while a lucky handful find fame and fortune, the rest of us quietly hone our crafts in unheralded

🖋 🖋 🖋 🖋 🖋 🖋 🖋 🖋

IF YOU GO:

City-Wide Open Studios *(203-772-2709; www.cwos.org) is held in October at a variety of venues in and around New Haven; the main exhibition is at Artspace, 50 Orange St. Most events are free.* **Getting there:** *From I-95 take exit 48 to I-91, then exit 3 (Trumbull Street). Turn left onto Orange Street, left onto Elm Street, right onto State Street, then right onto Crown Street. From the Merritt Parkway (CT 15) take exit 59; merge onto CT 69, turn right onto Whalley Avenue and follow it 3 miles, then merge onto Broadway, which turns into Elm Street. Turn right onto State Street, then right onto Crown Street.*

🖋 🖋 🖋 🖋 🖋 🖋 🖋 🖋

obscurity, in studios, lofts, and spare bedrooms. And like writing, making art can be a lonely, solitary existence. The studio tour allows them to show their work, maybe sell some of it, and meet like-minded folks all around them. "You'll see artists shaking hands for the first time," Kauder said of the Erector Square tenants, "even though they've worked together in those buildings for years."

Afterward, in one of New Haven's bustling coffeehouses, I raised my coffee cup to the city's thriving art scene and to Kauder, and toasted her for her vision, and her truly artful mind.

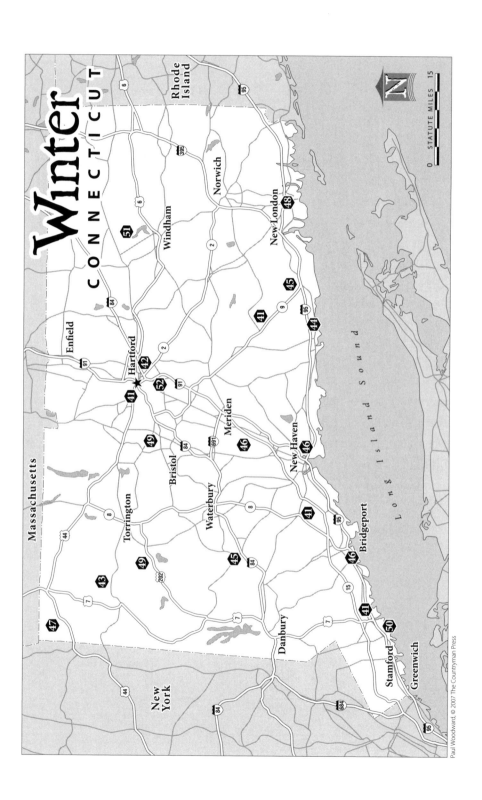

Winter

CONNECTICUT

Massachusetts

Rhode
Island

New
York

Enfield

Hartford

Torrington

Bristol

Waterbury

Meriden

Windham

Norwich

New London

New Haven

Danbury

Bridgeport

Stamford

Greenwich

Long Island Sound

N

0   STATUTE MILES   15

Paul Woodward, © 2007 The Countryman Press

Open Season
Historic Homes for the Holidays

The holidays can be stressful. Let Mark Twain describe it: "Xmas was invented to knock out the health & strength accumulated in the previous 11 months & shorten people's lives 10 per cent a year," he wrote to friend Lawrence Hutton in December 1892. "It does its work & accomplishes its mission with fiendish certainty."

Sound familiar? 'Tis the season for calling up memories of holidays past, but if there's no time or motivation to decorate your own place, worry not, because all around Connecticut, historic homes beckon, beautifully adorned for the season with doors open to visitors. What better time to take a well-deserved break from busy holiday schedules and treat ourselves to a glimpse at how the season was celebrated *long* long ago. Add the magic of a little snowfall, and you'll feel like you stepped into one of those snow globes with a fanciful little village inside.

Invitations like these, after all, come but once a year.

THE MARK TWAIN HOUSE AND MUSEUM, HARTFORD

Hartford is Twain Town, at least it was in the late 1800s, when Samuel Clemens, the writer and wit known to the world as Mark Twain, lived in a grand Victorian mansion in the city's Nook Farm neighborhood. Twain was one of the giants of 19th-century American literature, but when he was at home—*the* place for the author to unwind and enjoy time with his

Mark Twain's Victorian mansion in Hartford, decorated for the holidays

family—he just wanted to be ordinary. But the holidays—Christmastide, as it was called back then—was a decidedly over-the-top affair in the Twain household.

During the holiday season, the mansion is decorated as it was when Twain lived here with his wife, Livy, and daughters Jean, Clara, and Susy. China sparkles, silver shines, and holiday greenery adorns polished stair rails. Add designs by Louis Comfort Tiffany—antiques, chandeliers, gilded decor, and fine craftsmanship—and the scene is set for an authentic Victorian Christmas. It's so authentic, in fact, there's a palpable sense that the family will come rushing into the room at any moment. It's no accident: The curatorial staff uses information gleaned from Clemens family memorabilia, food and gift receipts, and correspondence.

"We take the family's own words so we know what they did," says Patti Phillipon, the museum's collections manager and exhibition coordinator. "The letters give great insight into what Sam Clemens and his family were like as people."

It's easy to imagine one of the world's greatest storytellers telling stories here, by a crackling fire or at the dinner table, set for one of the family's elaborate holiday meals. In the library, handmade ornaments and a half-strung popcorn-and-cranberry garland cover a table, as if the girls were just there. The guest room overflows with gift baskets similar to ones Livy delivered to friends and needy neighbors via horse-drawn sleigh on Christmas Eve. A Santa Claus suit is laid out on the billiard table in Twain's study, the cigar smoke–filled sanctuary where the youthful adventures of Huck Finn, Tom Sawyer, and other famous characters were brought to life.

"We try to show that he wasn't just this iconic American author; he was a man, too, with a family. He dressed up as Santa Claus and did all those things that most people do," Phillipon said. "It's kind of nice to see him as Sam Clemens the father and husband, as opposed to Mark Twain the author."

❅ ❅ ❅ ❅ ❅ ❅ ❅ ❅

IF YOU GO:

The Mark Twain House & Museum *(860-247-0998; www .marktwainhouse.org), 351 Farmington Ave., Hartford. Open Monday through Saturday 9:30–5:30; Sunday noon—5:30. Closed Tuesday January through April, and on major holidays. The house, open by guided tour, is decorated for the holidays from late November to early January. Next door, the $17 million state-of-the-art museum center is a spectacular shrine to all things Twain; a permanent exhibit in the Aetna Gallery explores his vast legacy.* **Getting there:** *Take I-84 to exit 46; follow Sisson Avenue to the end, then turn right onto Farmington Avenue; look for museum signs.*

❅ ❅ ❅ ❅ ❅ ❅ ❅ ❅

✽ ✽ ✽ ✽ ✽ ✽ ✽ ✽

MORE HOLIDAY HOUSE TOURS

Lockwood-Mathews Mansion Museum *(203-838-9799; www.lockwoodmathewsmansion.org), Mathews Park, 295 West Ave., Norwalk. Open Wednesday through Sunday noon–4; guided tours on the hour. The 62-room French Empire–style mansion of investment banker and railroad tycoon LeGrande Lockwood, built in 1864 for $2 million (about $200 million in 21st-century dollars), comes complete with soaring rotunda, frescoed walls, and elaborate woodwork. It's been lovingly restored to its original Victorian-era splendor, and during the holiday season, local designers transform the interior into a shimmering wonderland. History is alive here, and doesn't let you forget it.* **Getting there:** *exit 14 off I-95 north (exit 15 off I-95 south); follow West Avenue to the museum.*

Gillette Castle State Park *(860-526-2336; www.dep.state .ct.us/stateparks), 67 River Rd., East Haddam. Looming above the Connecticut River in East Haddam is the former home of stage actor and playwright William Gillette, best known for his portrayal of Sherlock Holmes. His role as the famous detective made him millions (back when there weren't many millionaires), much of which he spent building this retirement home-cum-medieval fortress-cum-castle, a monument to his flamboyant style or bad taste, depending on whom you ask. Whatever your take, most will agree it's a true Connecticut original. During the holiday season, the lavish interior is bedecked in the season's finery; it's open for tours on weekends from Thanksgiving to Christmas.* **Getting there:** *exit 69 off I-95 onto CT 9; take exit 7 and follow CT 82 to East Haddam; turn right onto River Road and follow it to the park.*

The Osborne Homestead Museum *(203-734-2513), Hawthorne Ave., Derby. Holiday house tours late November through mid-December, Thursday through Sunday 10–4. During the holiday season there are* *guided tours of the 1850 home of CEO and conservationist Frances Osborne Kellogg. The interior, full of fine art and antiques, is kept much as it was when she lived here in the early 20th century and is decorated in Victorian holiday finery.* **Getting there:** *Take CT 8 to exit 17; bear left and follow signs for Osbornedale State Park. Continue past the park onto Hawthorne Avenue; the house is on the left.*

New City, New Year

First Night Hartford

Hartford's annual New Year's Eve celebration was under way as usual, nearly 10 hours before the stroke of midnight. First Night organizers crossed their fingers and watched the sky as the snow and cold that blew in during the afternoon stretched into the evening. While the storm greatly diminished the size of the anticipated 30,000 crowd, the revelers who braved the elements to ring in the new year kept things lively. December 31st wouldn't be just another Saturday night in the capital city after all.

Art and culture take center stage in the city's official alcohol-free New Year's Eve party. A full roster of fun-for-the-family activities includes bands, storytellers, art exhibits, mask-making workshops, juggling—in all, dozens of events and performers—drawing crowds of admirers and giving people something fun to do downtown on the last night of the year.

Many wandered through a vacant Main Street storefront, which an encampment of local artists spent two days transforming into a work of art. Artist Jim Brunelle tapped into people's penchant for making promises by suspending hundreds of paper origami stars from the ceiling to create what he described as a "zone for mediation and introspection." It was the French painter Marcel Duchamp who said artists don't create art alone: The spectator contributes by deciphering and interpreting. Brunelle took that philosophy a step further.

"We wanted the piece to be interactive and participatory," he said, so instead of creating something for people to look at, he and fellow artists put out books, templates, scrolls, pens, and paper and encouraged visitors to have at it. Some people drew pictures while others wrote, reflecting on the year past or making resolutions for the soon-to-arrive one.

The result of artists spending a couple days in close confines is hard to predict, much like the creative process itself. "You take five or six artists and put them in a room together for 48 hours, and you don't know what's going to happen," event organizer Anne Cubberly noted. "And it's always amazing watching how people interact with art."

The 48 Hours of Art event fits squarely into the First Night concept that has grown in popularity since it debuted in Boston in 1976. That one was founded by local artists and residents as an alternative to the traditional boozy revelries that offered little in the way of family fun. Today, the Boston celebration attracts 1.5 million people and launched more than two hundred similar year-end fetes around the world.

Since 1988, First Night has been drawing huge crowds to Connecticut's capital city. This year's theme, "New City, New Year," is a nod both to the holiday and the city's downtown renaissance. "Hartford has a lot of new things going on, and First Night is part of that," said Becky Vortherms, the event's board president.

Hartford Guides dressed in red, white, and khaki were everywhere, assisting visitors and providing directions, and free shuttles whisked revelers between events. Music ran the gamut: At State House Square, the Nifty Fifties Band belted out doo-wop and Motown classics, and Last Fair Deal played old-time bluegrass, swing, and pop. Later on, Amy Gallatin & Stillwaters played "roots" music, a mix of vocals, fiddle, guitar, and acoustic bass, and a West Indian steel-drum band entertained those waiting for the 6 PM fireworks in Bushnell Park. And while the lively sound of steel drums is more white-sand-beach Caribbean than snowy-night New England, people dancing in the street didn't seem to notice, or care. There's nothing like hot Caribbean music to take the chill off.

In Bushnell Park, visitors undeterred by temperatures hovering around freezing gathered around an old-fashioned campfire, tended by area Boy Scouts so people could (what else) sing along to traditional American and Irish fireside tunes. Don Sineti and Steve Roys led the singing as pink-cheeked kids danced in the glow of the fire. Nearby, Keith Leaf wowed the crowd with a fiery performance, setting objects ablaze and juggling them, and kids spun around on the park's 1914 carousel, the magnificently carved horses keeping time to tunes blaring from the vintage Wurlitzer organ. A fortune-teller read tea leaves at City Hall, and Hartford Mayor Eddie Perez popped in at the austere Wadsworth Atheneum Museum of Art, where kids and their parents fashioned festive Mardi Gras–style masks out of paper, feathers, and beads.

The revelers that braved the deep freeze for the big moment were not disappointed. At midnight, bright bursts of fireworks shot into the sky over the city, heralding the first day of January. A long, cold winter loomed ahead, but for now there was the promise of a brand-new year uncluttered as yet with forgotten resolutions and the midwinter blahs.

A new year, after all, is a new chance at the art of living.

IF YOU GO:

First Night Hartford *(860-722-9546; www.firstnighthartford.org) takes place at nearly 20 indoor and outdoor downtown venues. Admission to all events is available with the purchase of a First Night button, available online and at various locations before New Year's Eve and at First Night.* **Getting there:** *Take any of the downtown Hartford exits off I-84 or I-91. Discounted parking is available at most parking garages.*

POWDER CHASE
Mohawk Mountain

My cousin Felicia and I had been talking all winter about downhill skiing. We somehow drifted away from the steep slopes over the years but, deciding it was time to relearn some old lessons, began planning our comeback. But where to? Everyone, it seemed, had an opinion: Killington. Stratton. Loon. Sugarloaf.

After all, who goes to Connecticut to ski, right? Surprise: We lit out not for the big boys up north, but for the hilly northwestern corner of the state. There are five mountains right here at home, easy jaunts from most anywhere, with a bonus: no predawn car trips, lights that come on at night so skiers don't fret when dusk starts to settle in late afternoon, and lift tickets that are generally lower than New England's well-known resorts. Add lots of weekday specials, and you have yourself a bargain.

A word about Connecticut's winter playgrounds: You won't find western-style double-black-diamond runs, or megaresorts with trailside condos and après scene. These are family-friendly, close-knit affairs where lift lines are blessedly short, terrain is forgiving, and trails number in the dozens rather than the hundreds. And for skiers looking to learn the sport, try snowboarding for the first time, or, in our case, tune up their downhill technique, therein lies the appeal.

We settled on Cornwall's Mohawk Mountain, whose 1,600-foot elevation is Connecticut's loftiest skiing terrain. Plus, when you ski here you

Fresh snow on Mohawk Mountain

are a part of history, and nobody knows this better than Carol Lugar, whose life has been intertwined with the mountain ever since her father, National Ski Hall of Famer Walt Schoenknecht, opened the state's first ski area here in the 1940s. Today, she's the president of the family business, and has witnessed the advent of everything from snowboarding and high-performance fabrics (think microfleece and Gore-Tex) to the shaped skis favored by rusty skiers revisiting a sport left behind long ago.

"They're perfect for someone like you," Lugar reassured me when I admitted to my decade-plus hiatus.

Clicked into bindings, we shuffled toward the lift, and in minutes we were above the slopes where, as youngsters, we learned to snowplow and face plant. Gray clouds scuttled across the cobalt sky as we huddled against the prickly touch of wind-blown snow coming off the mountain. We watched skiers making long, graceful arcs and winced as a snowboarder took a spectacular tumble and disappeared in a poof of white powder.

On the map, we studied the greens, blues, and diamonds—24 in all—and decided on Deer Run, a gently meandering novice trail. "Last one down's a coward!" I issued the challenge as we assumed snowplow position and pushed down on our poles. I cautiously initiated my first turn on the bulletproof hard pack; below me, Felicia wobbled but quickly recovered. The skiers flying by us, I noted, were really, really small. The fact that four-year-olds were gliding by on either side didn't embarrass us. Not. At. All. Soon enough, however, we were moving along at a good clip. It felt good to dig my edges, link one turn after another, and find a rhythm. Smiling the rest of the way down, I stopped at the bottom and looked back up the trail. Somehow, incredibly, I'd actually done it.

Back on the lift, pink-cheeked and happy, we compared notes and consulted the map. We eliminated the black-diamond express to the bottom, eyeing instead the blue squares marking the intermediate trails. I

❄ ❄ ❄ ❄ ❄ ❄ ❄ ❄

MORE DOWNHILL SKIING

Ski Sundown *(860-379-7669; www.skisundown.com), 126 Ratlum Rd., New Hartford*

Mount Southington Ski Area *(860-628-0954; 1-800-982-6828; www.mountsouthington.com), 396 Mount Vernon Rd., Southington*

Woodbury Ski Area *(203-263-2203; www.woodburyskiarea.com), 785 Washington Rd. (CT 47), Woodbury*

❄ ❄ ❄ ❄ ❄ ❄ ❄ ❄

IF YOU GO:

Mohawk Mountain *(860-672-6100; 1-800-895-5222; www.mohawkmtn.com), 46 Great Hollow Rd., Cornwall.* **Getting there:** *From Hartford take I-84 west to exit 39; follow CT 4 west to Cornwall.*

filled Felicia in on the legend of Walt Schoenknecht; how—thanks to his pioneering forays into snowmaking—ski areas are no longer at the mercy of fickle New England winters. And at Mount Snow—the venerable Vermont resort he founded in the 1950s—he developed more firsts, like high-capacity chairlifts and extra-wide trails.

We spent the rest of the day on the blues, starting with Arrow Head. Felicia went first, getting smaller and smaller as she made crisp, tight turns. I took a last look at the backdrop of snow-covered Berkshires and pointed my skis down the hill. I came off each turn with a little push, coaxing myself faster as my confidence rose, ending the run at the back of the line with a neat *swoosh.*

Mohawk's niche is well defined—the mountain attracts 100,000 visitors every season, primarily kids and their families, and on weekday afternoons schoolchildren arrive by the busload. "There's a family mentality because we're family-run," Lugar said. "We have fourth-generation skiers here, people who learned to ski and stayed, or came back when they had kids."

We sipped cocoa in the 1940s-era Pine Lodge, and when the warmth of this ski lodge staple coursed down to our toes, we were good for a couple more runs. Skiing happily along, we reeled in some snowboarders, wishing we could go on for miles. As the lights flickered on, an obliging skier snapped our photo, the mountain looming behind us in the twilight. It would be hard to imagine a nicer day.

On the back-roads drive home I replayed those smooth turns down Arrow Head. I didn't tackle the steep chutes, but, safely in my comfort zone, relived the thrill that comes from a decent run down a mountain. Suddenly all my solid reasons for not skiing seemed like a collection of flimsy excuses. I realize that, like shaped skis, Connecticut's slopes are a perfect fit for someone like me.

THE CALL OF THE OUTLET MALL

It's cold. It gets dark early. Snow blankets the ground and swirls in the frigid air. What a perfect time to search for that certain something that will take the chill off while making us smile, maybe even stylish. Shopping is a four-season sport, of course, but there's nothing like a bargain to help us brave—maybe even enjoy—the winter weeks to come.

Who among us doesn't love a bargain? Not me, that's for sure. Because, in point of fact, I can't afford the $800 price tag of a pair of Chanel leather boots. Unless, of course, I can score a really good deal. That's where outlet shopping comes in.

If you're living (and shopping) on less, more people than you think are in your shoes—fabulous shoes, if they're shopping at outlets, where top retailers offer designer deals, cute clothes, and fancy bling for people who want to enrich their wardrobe with capital-S style without dropping big bucks on up-to-the-minute trends (like the jersey knit dresses and platform pumps that are big at the moment).

I stopped hearing the call of the mall long ago. In my teenage years I was as hard-core a shopper as they come; as an adult with less money and time for shopping, the mind-numbing crowds just left me dazed and drained. I made a pact: No more mind-numbing mall shopping for me.

Sound familiar?

Then a wonderful thing happened in Connecticut. The outlets came,

Outlet shopping along the shore

and while Maine is decidedly the outlet-shopping capital of New England, Connecticut offers upscale bargain hunting that's popular among those of us looking for deals on designer duds at discount prices. So with a never-pay-full-price mantra and a comfy pair of walking shoes, I headed toward the shore, where outlet malls are bona fide tourist destinations in their own right, especially on rainy beach days. The destination: Clinton Crossing Premium Outlets in Clinton.

One thing made itself readily clear: This was not the same experience that I remembered as a young shopper; you know, when it meant picking up jeans, sneakers, and windbreakers (with imperfections, in many cases) at rock-bottom prices. "Outlet shopping has become far more sophisticated," general manager Robyn Rifkin told me. "As people's tastes have become more sophisticated, companies have had to rise to the occasion."

HOW TO BE A
SMART OUTLET SHOPPER

Do you consider yourself a bargain hunter? Can you sniff out a deal? If not, a few tips will point you in the right direction. Here's a strategy:

• Shop with a plan. Don't wander around aimlessly, which wastes time and money. A short list of three or four stores will fill an afternoon and help you avoid spur-of-the-moment purchases.

• Shop in the clearance sections; it's like getting a double discount.

• Know your prices. If you do some homework, you'll know when a deal is really a deal. Checking popular discount shopping Web sites (www.shopping.com, www.shopzilla.com, www.sortprice.com) is like window shopping at home.

• Avoid peak shopping hours; quiet times are generally early morning midweek.

• Many shopping outlets offer their own coupon books available for purchase. Stop in at the mall's management office; Clinton Crossing's VIP Coupon Book costs $5 and includes most of the shops.

• Time your purchases. Sign up for your favorite store's in-store mailing list; it will give you a heads-up on coupons and upcoming sales.

If you come to the outlets in search of upscale, swanky versions of ordinary stuff (think 1,000-thread count sheets and Henckels knives), you're in the right place. And if you must wear Armani or Versace, for Pete's sake, don't pay full price. The 70 boutique-style specialty shops are stocked with clearance items right from the parent chain. If you love the thrill of the hunt, merchandise is always changing: some past season, some irregular or overstock, all direct from the manufacturer or the full-price store. For shoppers, that means amazing deals; even deals on deals, as is often the case.

So I began at Barneys New York, where the first thing that caught my eye was a $125 Juicy Couture velour hoodie for $43. Folded primly on a nearby table was a $200 cashmere cardigan for $99. Under a sign touting "Fab New Shoes," I found a strappy pair of $465 hot pink Manolo Blahniks for $220. In the Off 5th Saks Fifth Avenue outlet, silk Versace neckties retailing for $120 were half the price, and a funky pair of Allen B. jewel-encrusted jeans were a bargain at $159 (retail $350). Kate Spade handbags were a good deal, too.

One last insider tip: While everyday discounts range from 25 to 65 percent off retail, it serves a smart shopper well to seek out the sales upon sales (usually going on in the back of the store). On my visit, drastic markdowns were being drastically marked down, meaning huge potential savings.

Outlets provide the rush that only comes from buying costly items for a fraction of their retail price. And the bonus? One-stop bargain shopping fits neatly into our time-strapped lives. Sure I daydream about shopping Fifth Avenue—and so do you. But frugal shoppers know that you can dress like a fashionista without letting the world in on how little you've paid.

❄ ❄ ❄ ❄ ❄ ❄ ❄ ❄

IF YOU GO

Clinton Crossing Premium Outlets *(860-664-0700; www .premiumoutlets.com/Clinton), 20-A Killingworth Turnpike (CT 81), Clinton.* **Getting there:** *From I-95 take exit 63 to CT 81.*

MORE OUTLET SHOPPING

Tanger Outlet Center *(860-399-8656; 1-866-665-8685; www.tangeroutlet.com), 314 Flat Rock Place, Westbrook. More than 65 designer outlet stores and brand-name manufacturers offering savings up to 40 percent off retail.* **Getting there:** *exit 65 off I-95.*

❄ ❄ ❄ ❄ ❄ ❄ ❄ ❄

EYEING BALD EAGLES

You never know what the sight of a bald eagle will do to people seeing one for the first time in the wild. Some whoop, others cry, and a few are rendered speechless. At least that's what happened on my first eagle-viewing trip. Me, I tried to absorb every detail—the yellow beak, the cocoa-brown body, the easy-to-spot white head and tail—as I peered through my binoculars at the majestic creature wheeling high over the Connecticut River.

But this much is certain: The not-to-be-missed sight of a soaring bald eagle should be on every nature lover's to-do list. In Connecticut, there are two hot spots where America's symbol of freedom likes to roost, fly, and fish—the open waters of the lower Connecticut River and at the Shepaug Dam on the Housatonic River in Southbury—destinations that offer a rare chance to point binoculars and camera lenses at the water, the sky, and the treetops for glimpses of the northern bald eagles now a regular part of the state's winter bird population.

I drove down to Essex on a chilly Tuesday morning in February, to where Captain Mark Yuknat had the 54-foot *RiverQuest* idling at Steamboat Dock. Soon we were motoring up New England's longest waterway, whose name in the Mohegan Indian language means "the long tidal river," not far from where it spills into Long Island Sound. Thanks to tidal action and warm temperatures, there's plenty of the ice-free open

MARK YUKNAT

Wintering bald eagles on the Connecticut River

water that eagles need to feed on fish and fowl. The plan: Search for the 80 or so eagles here from the frozen north (in this case, upstate New York, northern New England, and Canada); in all, a two-hour tour of one of the largest concentrations of wintering bald eagles on the East Coast.

For many, the river journey is a feel-good occasion that reaffirms the eagles' remarkable comeback. In 1782, they became the national emblem of the upstart United States, but the outlook was grim 30 years ago, when *Haliaeetus leucocephalus* was on the brink of extinction, thanks in no small part to DDT and other pesticides. Fast forward to 2006: Not only are these majestic birds nesting and raising eaglets in Connecticut, but the U.S. Fish and Wildlife Service is considering their removal from the federal list of threatened species.

The eagles were right on cue. We saw our first one within minutes, an adult cruising low over the water. "Here he is!" someone shouted. As everyone fumbled for field glasses and telephoto camera lenses, two more came into view, soaring and swooping above the river in a magnificent aerial display.

Winter is a stressful time for eagles, so Captain Mark kept a comfortable distance as *RiverQuest* crunched through thin ice floes. James Restivo, a Connecticut Audubon Society naturalist, briefed us on how to use clues to determine age: A buff-colored body with white plumage marks a juvenile; it takes five years for adults to come by the distinctive white head and dark brown body.

In what would become a familiar pattern, the trip brought one amazing sight after another. An adult hunting alone, circling farther and farther into the sky. A pair, executing some spectacularly coordinated aerial moves. Courtship? Territorial wrangling? Play? I didn't know what they were up to, nor did I care. I was just thrilled to have a front seat to the pas de deux. Another came to light on a spindly branch; based on its plumage and my newfound know-how, I judged it to be a juvenile. It took off after

---

❄ ❄ ❄ ❄ ❄ ❄ ❄ ❄

IF YOU GO

Connecticut River Expeditions *(860-662-0577; reservations: 1-800-996-8747; www.ctriverexpeditions.org) offers eagle viewing along the lower Connecticut River from February to mid-March aboard* RiverQuest, *leaving from Steamboat Dock at the Connecticut River Museum in Essex.* **Getting there:** *exit 3 off CT 9; follow the signs to Essex.*

The Connecticut Audubon Society Eagle Festival *(203-259-6305; boat reservations: 1-800-714-7201; www.ctaudubon.org), Main St., Essex. In February, this bald eagle bash, the largest birding festival in North America, celebrates the return of wintering bald eagles to the Connecticut River with eagle-viewing boat trips, birds-of-prey demonstrations, and other eco-friendly events.*

❄ ❄ ❄ ❄ ❄ ❄ ❄ ❄

a kingfisher, then set its massive wings and rode the air currents in huge, lazy circles above us. As I latched onto his movements with my binoculars, someone gave me an excited nudge: A red-tailed hawk and a young eagle were swooping and diving over Hamburg Cove. We were spellbound.

On the return trip, I checked my tally—twenty-five eagles, not a bad day. I may have counted the same eagle twice, and, again, I didn't care. And when we thought it couldn't possibly get better, a pair of adults were seen watching us from their nest high above Nott Island. As they took turns cutting graceful arcs above us, I made a mental note to freeze this day in the memory bank. The deck was pin-drop quiet until a woman's voice broke the silence. "Spectacular," she whispered, teary-eyed behind binoculars. "Just spectacular." Our guide, who makes the trip a few times a week, shared the awe. "That was one of the best shows you can expect to see on the river," James said, although surely everyone already figured as much. "It's hard to become complacent about bald eagles."

MORE EAGLES

*The **Shepaug Eagle Observation Area** (1-800-368-8954), Shepaug Hydroelectric Station, River Road, Southbury, is open from late December to mid-March, Wednesday, Saturday, and Sunday. 9–1. Admission is free, but reservations are required. Another spot wintering bald eagles find to their liking is the Housatonic River at the hydro station in Southbury, where the churning water stays clear of ice and eagles like to perch, fish, and fly. An observation hut overlooking the Shepaug Dam has high-powered telescopes at the ready and volunteer naturalists on hand to help spot the eagles. **Getting there:** exit 13 off I-84; follow River Road to the observation area.*

TRAVELS WITH TYKES

Connecticut's Family-Friendly Fun Spots

Yup, the cliché is true: The family that plays together, stays together. But the two of you love history, while the kids are strictly into 21st-century diversions. What's a fun-challenged family to do?

If you've got youngsters in tow, visit some of Connecticut's kid-friendly hot spots. Fun, of course, knows no age, and the following attractions conjure up enough magic to ignite excitement in the most jaded adult. Together, they're a veritable gold mine of fun for children, places where their curiosity is satisfied and the whole family can learn something new.

CONNECTICUT'S BEARDSLEY ZOO, BRIDGEPORT

The woman at the ticket window handed me a map and urged me to see the entire menagerie of wild things—more than 300 in all, representing 125 species—but especially the tiger cubs. "They're almost as big as mom now," she said proudly.

It was the kind of crisp, clear morning that precedes a nor'easter, which, incidentally, was on the way, and perhaps explained why I was the sole visitor at Connecticut's only zoo. My first stop: face time with an Andean condor, one of the world's largest flying birds. While I couldn't be sure why he displayed his 10-foot wingspan, I preferred to interpret it as a friendly greeting. With a beady little eye, a turkey vulture gave me the avian equivalent of a dirty look. "Keep it moving," the expression suggested. By the time the timber wolf trotted over, one thing became clear: When you're the only human around, animals take note. I had to remind myself that he was a wild predator and not a friendly mutt.

It doesn't take long to appreciate the added bonus of a winter visit: Without summer's heat and humidity, the animals are quite lively. "I always tell people, 'Come back in January,'" said Jessica Summers, the zoo's development director. The North American species particularly love the cold. "In August, the animals are as hot as we are."

The up-close look at native wildlife was a treat. A red fox blinked a few times before sauntering off, unimpressed by my presence. Delightfully curious, however, was the white-tailed deer that followed me along the fence line, and a barred owl that stared with saucer-shaped eyes. The re-created rain forest was a ticket to the tropics, the steaminess a pleasant shock in the midst of a Connecticut winter. Everywhere, little scenes exploded into life—poison dart frogs, rainbow keel-billed toucans, and howler monkeys shrieked and scampered, while exotic birds soared through the free-flight aviary. Know what a broad-snouted caiman looks like? Neither did I, but I found it, perfectly camouflaged, playing nature's hide-and-seek game.

While the typical zoo is about animals, animals, and more animals, here visitors can see the Bard's classics at a summertime Shakespeare festival, ride a historic carousel, and visit the Victorian greenhouse (the zoo was founded in 1875). "Big-city zoos are great, but families like the fact that they don't have to travel far or spend big money when they come here," said Summers, noting that it takes about three hours to see everything.

I saved the big cats for last. She was right—at first, I couldn't distinguish Viktor, Koshka, and Nika from their mother, a magnificent Siberian tiger named Anastasia. But despite the imposing size and gleaming white teeth that betray their status as one of the world's most fearsome predators, their silly antics were all cub.

Children love the Peabody Museum of Natural History at Yale.

MELANIE BRIGOCKAS

BARKER CHARACTER, COMIC & CARTOON MUSEUM, CHESHIRE

Attention nostalgia fans (and aren't we all?): This one-of-a-kind treasure is a trove of happy childhood memories, a century of cartoon history, and a shrine to popular culture, rolled into one.

"A lot of kids have to take a step back," museum director Nancy Spitzer explained as she led us through rooms crammed, literally, to the rafters. "It's a bombardment of the senses."

This applies to kids of all ages, of course. Like the 88-year-old visitor who spotted the museum's 19th-century Yellow Kid gumball machine. "I watched every wrinkle fall from her face," recalled Spitzer, "she was an eight-year-old girl again."

Spitzer calls such times "goose-bump moments," and they happen often. "Your toys are your history," she noted. "When you want to go to a happy place, that's what you remember."

Herb and Gloria Barker's whimsical hobby evolved into the largest museum of its kind in New England, a staggering collection of 80,000 items amassed, at first, anyway, from yard sales and consignment shops. No admission is charged, and nothing is for sale. It's all here: lunch boxes, board games, treasures from gumball machines and cereal boxes. An entire room devoted to Pez dispensers. Fictional characters made famous in comic strips and films, television commercials, and advertising campaigns. The 21st century is also well represented (warning: kids will make a beeline for the Pixar and Harry Potter collectibles).

Your inner child might squeal with delight upon sight of Mr. Potato Head, but Lisa spotted a Donny & Marie vinyl lunchbox, and high on a shelf, my favorite Tweety Bird drinking glass, collected from Burger King in the 1970s. I made a mental note to tell my parents about the Lone Ranger flashlight ring and Joe Palooka boxing gloves.

Duly enchanted, we passed the drive home recalling childhood memories of favorite board games and 3-D View-Masters, Cracker Jack prizes, and Raggedy Ann dolls, the stuff of childhood dreams.

❋ ❋ ❋ ❋ ❋ ❋ ❋ ❋

IF YOU GO:

Connecticut's Beardsley Zoo *(203-394-6565; www.beardsley zoo.org), 1875 Noble Ave., Bridgeport. Open daily 9–4.* **Getting there:** *Follow CT 8 south to exit 5 in Bridgeport, bear right onto Boston Avenue, then turn left at the fifth traffic light onto Noble Avenue.*

Barker Character, Comic & Cartoon Museum *(203-699-3822; www.barkermuseum.com), 1188 Highland Ave. (CT 10), Cheshire. Open Wednesday through Saturday 11–5.* **Getting there:** *exit 3 off I-691, follow CT 10 to the museum.*

Peabody Museum of Natural History *(203-432-5050; www.peabody.yale.edu), 170 Whitney Ave., New Haven. Open Monday through Saturday 10–5; Sunday noon–5; closed major holidays.* **Getting there:** *From I-91 take exit 3 onto the Trumbull Street connector, then turn right onto Whitney Avenue.*

❋ ❋ ❋ ❋ ❋ ❋ ❋ ❋

PEABODY MUSEUM OF NATURAL HISTORY, NEW HAVEN

The ancient skeletons loomed overhead while Janet Roberts regaled us with knowledge gleaned from years spent guiding wide-eyed children (and adults) through the Great Hall of Dinosaurs. *They* seemed to be listening, too, as if to hear what docents say about them. Like the juvenile *Apatosaurus*, for instance, the largest mounted dinosaur in a museum famous for its dinosaurs. Or *Deinonychus*, poised in attack mode. And *Archelon*, the largest-ever species of turtle, which likely weighed in at 3 tons when it inhabited the Cretaceous seas.

In 1866, O. C. Marsh founded the Peabody, whose 13 million specimens and artifacts include the internationally known fossils the Yale paleontologist discovered and named—*Triceratops*, *Stegosaurus*, and *Apatosaurus* (aka *Brontosaurus*) among them.

None whip youngsters into a frenzy quite like *Tyrannosaurus rex*.

"Although *Allosaurus* is much nastier, for its size," Roberts said. Her favorite? *Stegosaurus.* "He's just so peculiar, with his huge plates, spiked tail, and tiny head."

Above us stretched the 1940s-era Pulitzer-winning *Age of Reptiles* mural, a 300-million-year-long panorama of reptilian life on earth. Impressive, certainly, but kids like to touch stuff, so Roberts produced a lumpy object from her fossil cart and passed it around. "Coprolite," she explained, "probably left behind by a saber-toothed tiger about 10 million years ago." Petrified dung is of special interest, she said, since it reveals not only what animals ate long ago, but often what the climate was like. "Cool," a boy in our group whispered, seconds before his mom whisked him toward the bathroom and, based on her dour expression, the soap.

❋ ❋ ❋ ❋ ❋ ❋ ❋ ❋

MORE FAMILY FUN

Stepping Stones Museum for Children *(203-899-0606; www.steppingstonesmuseum.org), Mathews Park, 303 West Ave., Norwalk*

Children's Museum of Southeastern Connecticut *(860-691-1111; www.childrensmuseumsect.org), 409 Main St., Niantic*

Dinosaur State Park *(860-529-8423; www.dinosaurstatepark.org), 400 West St., Rocky Hill*

Kidcity Children's Museum *(860-347-0495; www.kidcity museum.com), 119 Washington St., Middletown*

See also **Connecticut Science Center** *(chapter 8)*

❋ ❋ ❋ ❋ ❋ ❋ ❋ ❋

KINGS AND QUEENS OF THE HILL

The Salisbury Ski Jumping Championships

The first question ski jumping outsiders might ask is "Why?" Why would people strap on skis and launch themselves headlong into the air? And how do they end the run on their feet?

But the jumper from Lake Placid made it look so easy. She simply accelerated down the 300-foot-long ramp, took flight at around 50 miles per hour, then floated back to earth, where her skis touched down with a clean *smack* on the packed snow, speeding through a flurry of ringing cowbells, long, golden braid trailing behind.

The girl in bib number 53 was tiny, and astonishingly young, I marveled, trying to remember what I was up to when *I* was 11. Certainly nothing half so gutsy, I thought ruefully. Her 46.5-meter practice jump was, so far, the second-longest jump of the day in the women's category of the Salisbury Invitational Ski Jump.

Winter in Connecticut conjures up visions of snowshoeing, skating ponds, and UConn basketball. But ski jumps? I wondered about that when I first heard of the competition a decade or so ago. Salisbury is a well-known center for competitive ski jumping, where the bravest of the brave launch themselves from Satre Memorial Hill for two days every February. The annual event in this little colonial town has taken place since 1926, making it one of the oldest such competitions in the country. Even if you're not a fan of ski jumping, consider this beloved winter fixture a must-see event.

Ski jumping has been a Salisbury tradition since the 1920s.

Salisbury's legendary hill is the only ski jump in Connecticut, and one of the few left in New England, but the sport is alive and well in the rural northwest corner, where all ages take flight, thanks to a dedicated cadre of volunteers. Many boast direct ties to the immigrants who brought the sport to town in the 1920s from their native Norway, Olympic ski jumping's most decorated nation. The Salisbury Winter Sports Association, a local group dedicated to the tradition of Nordic skiing, offers jumping, cross-country skiing, and alpine skiing programs for local youngsters.

The hill is full of stories, of the days when they jumped on wooden skis, before brightly colored body suits, helmets, and state-of-the-art equipment was the norm. It all began, the story goes, when Norwegian immigrant John Satre (pronounced SAY-tree) climbed atop a shed with skis strapped to his feet and jumped. In time, the current 64-meter tower was built, tucked into the pines just outside the village center.

And with this being an Olympic year, spirits were especially high. While ski jumping's biggest names were competing in the Olympic Winter Games in the Italian Alps, Satre Hill was packed with an enthusiastic crowd of locals and weekenders bundled in their best outerwear to see talented jumpers from around the Northeast catch big air, and hoping to witness the shattering of the hill's jump record—an amazing 231 feet—in a sport that takes an equal measure of strength, coordination, and courage.

One by one, jumpers had spectators looking at the sky, soaring as much as 200 feet above the crowd in the aerodynamic V-shaped position that dates to the 1950s—arms pinned against their sides and leaning far forward over their ski tips, gliding gracefully through the air before touching earth again.

Jumpers are scored with a formula that combines distance with style points. Judges scrutinize each performance for the elements of a perfect flight: fluidity, control, precision, a smooth telemark-style landing (one foot in front of the other, arms up, and skis parallel), and where they land in relation to the hill's red zone—called the K-Point. "It's not how long you make it," the announcer explained to the crowd. "It's how you make it long."

And there were many long jumps, one after another, it seemed. The crowd was loving it, ringing cowbells furiously as one jumper after another soared off the tower and seemed to float through the air in perfect precision before touching down and speeding through the landing area.

I thought of the crowds at Torino and was happy to be here instead, where everyone seemed to know each other. After all, half of Salisbury, it is said, works at the jumps, and the other half comes to watch up-and-comers dreaming of gold—perhaps at the 2010 Olympics—and mingle with past jumpers representing a who's who of American ski jumping. Like Salisbury's Roy Sherwood, the former Olympian and U.S. ski jumping champion considered the best American jumper of his generation, who learned to jump on Satre Hill. About a dozen people stood around the fire pit, kicking at the logs and sending sparks into the air. The question rippling through the crowd was: Will they jump tomorrow? At the moment, a nor'easter was roaring up the East Coast, expected to dump a couple feet of snow between now and tomorrow's U.S. Eastern National Championships. For now, the announcer proclaimed it an exceptional day of ski jumping, recounted the winners, and added a bit of advice: "Watch for these names in Vancouver."

IF YOU GO:

The **Salisbury Winter Sports Association** *(860-435-0019; www.swsa.info) hosts the Salisbury Invitational Ski Jump and U.S. Eastern National Championships every February on Satre Hill. Morning practice runs are followed by competition that begins each day at 1 PM.* **Getting there:** *Take US 44 from the east, US 41 from western Massachusetts, or US 7 from I-95 to the center of Salisbury.*

SUBMARINE STATE

Historic Ship *Nautilus* and Submarine Force Museum

WHAT ONE MAN CAN IMAGINE, ANOTHER CAN ACHIEVE. So reads the script swirling over the entryway of the U.S. Navy's Submarine Force Museum in Groton, whose showpiece is the USS *Nautilus*.

They are the words of Jules Verne, the French writer whose fantasies of emerging technology and undersea adventure—to wit, his seminal novel *Twenty Thousand Leagues Under the Sea*—would become reality nearly a century later.

It was almost 10 on a Wednesday morning in late February, and 50-mile-per-hour gusts were blowing up whitecaps on the Thames River. Still, I was expecting a crowd at the *Nautilus*. This is, after all, a naval submarine base in a city known as the Submarine Capital of America.

But as I crossed the bow of the historic ship submerged in the icy river, a young officer delivered the news. "You're the only one here today," he said, handing me an audio wand for the self-guided recorded tour. "Have fun."

Only one? Surely I heard him wrong. But sure enough, I descend the long, narrow flight of stairs belowdecks and found . . . no one. I had the world's first nuclear-powered submarine to myself.

So I set to the task at hand—exploring the 362-foot sub's cylindrical-shaped interior, divided into a tight maze of narrow corridors, steep

The Submarine Force Museum

staircases, and low doorways—amazed that one hundred men once journeyed beneath the sea in these close confines. Mannequins dressed up as frozen-in-time submariners really seem to be on duty: peering into a periscope, dining in the officers' quarters, filing the ship's correspondence, listening through headphones in the sonar room.

The attack center is outfitted with everything needed to defend the boat, including the firing panel used to launch torpedoes. The control room has the long-range sonar, sophisticated communications, and precise navigation needed for diving, surfacing, and controlling the ship that revolutionized naval warfare.

It was not long after World War II when Admiral Hyman G. Rickover, the "Father of the Nuclear Navy," led engineers and research scientists in developing a sub fueled by the atom. Its keel was laid by Harry Truman in 1952, then christened by Mamie Eisenhower and launched into the Thames in 1954—the same year, incidentally, that Walt Disney Pictures released the movie version of Verne's *Nautilus* tale. In 1955, Commander Eugene P. Wilkinson famously declared "Under way on nuclear power," and the lines of the newly commissioned sub were officially cast.

The "shark of steel" put the Navy at the top of its game, a marvel of weaponry and electronics fueled by a nuclear reactor that provided steam to drive the electric generators and main engines. It could slip silently into the ocean and cruise faster and longer than diesel-powered subs, shattering speed and distance records: Its 1,300-mile maiden voyage to San Juan took less than four days, farther and faster than a submarine had ever traveled. After logging half a million miles, the *Nautilus* was retired, designated a National Historic Landmark, and brought home to Connecticut.

It's easy to lose track of time underwater, apparently, and eventually an officer came down to the crew mess to check on me. Some people get claustrophobic in cramped confines, he explained, and I had been down there awhile. Now that he mentioned it, the stormy waters were rocking the sub, or were they? "It's tied up pretty good, right?" I asked, trying to sound casual, picturing the gusts and the whitecaps. "Yes," he answered patiently, in the kind of tone usually reserved for addressing small children or the very, very old.

Back on land, I marveled at the displays of Cold War–era combat systems, and the submarine rescue chamber used to save 33 crewmen when the USS *Squalus* sank off the coast of New Hampshire in 1939. Exhibits and documentary-style videos tell the story of the Navy's "silent service," from the Revolutionary War–era *Turtle* (developed by Connecticut's own David Bushnell) to modern subs like the *Seawolf*, and decades of weapons systems technology.

The museum complex sees 150,000 visitors a year, a mix of war veterans, former submariners and their families, schoolchildren, and the curious just wandering off I-95. In 2005 the sub base was on the Pentagon's proposed list of closings, but members of the state's congressional delegation lobbied hard—and successfully—to reverse the decision (the base brings in about $2.5 billion in state revenue). Downstream, Connecticut's defense industry manifests itself at General Dynamics Corp.'s Electric Boat shipyard, where state and national dignitaries gathered in 2006 to witness the launch of the country's newest *Virginia*-class submarine, the *Hawaii*, with a spray of champagne and a traditional Hawaiian blessing. It was the 100th nuclear-powered submarine delivered by Electric Boat to the U.S. Navy.

Driving away, I envisioned not the torpedoes, periscopes, and ballast tanks below the surface, but a book displayed behind glass in the officers' wardroom. It was the 19th-century edition of Verne's novel, presented to Commander William Anderson when the sub arrived in France, and opened to an illustration of Captain Nemo at the wheel of its namesake. I took a last look at the sleek sub quietly at rest in the Thames, an idea ahead of its time, brought to life.

❋ ❋ ❋ ❋ ❋ ❋ ❋ ❋

IF YOU GO:

Submarine Force Museum *(860-694-3174; 1-800-343-0079; www.ussnautilus.org), One Crystal Lake Rd., off CT 12, Groton. Open May through October, Wednesday through Monday 9–5, Tuesday 1–5; November through May, Wednesday through Monday 9–4; closed Tuesday, Thanksgiving, Christmas, and New Year's Day. Free admission.* **Getting there:** *From I-95 take exit 86 and follow the signs to the museum.*

❋ ❋ ❋ ❋ ❋ ❋ ❋ ❋

CROSS-COUNTRY SKIING
White Memorial and Winding Trails

Winter. This is New England's season, a time of bundling up, hunkering down, and hoping for the first flakes of a new storm. But while many say light the fire, skiers say let it snow. If you get cabin fever—and who doesn't?—don't succumb to the cold-weather blues. Fight back! Snow is an open invitation to get outside and play. There's nothing like the white stuff to put you in a winter mood, and exercise and fresh air to fend off the winter blues. Cross-country skiing uses more of your own steam than swooshing down a mountain at breakneck speeds. No time to head north? In-the-know-skiers are satisfied in Connecticut. There aren't a lot of ski facilities, per se. And yet, despite that, or perhaps because of it, the cross-country skiing is excellent. A word of note: This being southern New England, cross-country skiing in our state is touch and go. Some years don't offer much. But when it's good, it's really good.

When the rest of Connecticut is drowning in rain, the Litchfield Hills are often covered in snow, including the **White Memorial Foundation**, a vast 4,000-acre tract spread across Litchfield and Morris that's a popular winter destination for the outdoorsy set. Its 30 miles of trails and old woods roads provide a wide range of terrain to accommodate skiers of all levels. This is a no-frills kind of ski experience, which means no warming huts, equipment rentals, or ski lodge, just a pristine landscape of forest, meadows, and wetlands that is always open.

A late-night snowfall left a fresh blanket of powdery snow that glittered like diamonds in the early-morning light. As we glide along a silent trail beneath snowcapped evergreens, the woods are pin-drop quiet (during the week, it's not unheard of to enjoy solitary runs down deserted trails), and we look for signs of the deer, fox, wild turkeys, and bobcats that roam the dense forests and open fields. Our route takes us past frozen ponds, streams, and Bantam Lake, the largest natural lake in Connecticut.

It's been one of those New England winters: Snow has been iffy, and Connecticut has been hurting for the white stuff. Skiers ventured into an uncertain season with the warmest January on record, but a February nor'easter promised to turn it around, so when I called **Winding Trails Cross-Country Ski Center** soon after the season's first decent storm, I was surprised by the news. "We got two feet of snow last weekend," Scott Brown, the center's director, said. "But we lost it as quickly as we got it."

This ski haven tucked into the suburbs west of Hartford has, as its

IF YOU GO:

White Memorial Foundation *(860-567-0857; www.white memorialcc.org), 80 Whitehall Rd., off US 202, Litchfield. Grounds open dawn to dusk. Several trails head into the woods near the junction of CT 61 and 63, along White's Woods Road; or start at the museum at the main entrance, where you can pick up a trail map of the property.* **Getting there:** *The main entrance is off US 202 in Litchfield, about 2 miles west of the green.*

Winding Trails Cross Country Ski Center *(860-674-4227; www.windingtrails.com), 50 Winding Trails Dr. (off CT 4), Farmington.* **Getting there:** *exit 39 off I-84; follow CT 4 through Farmington; turn right onto Devonwood Drive, then take the first left onto Winding Trails Drive.*

Skiing through a meadow at White Memorial in Litchfield

* * * * * * * *

MORE SKIING

Woodbury Ski Area *(203-263-2203; www.woodburyskiarea.com),
785 Washington Rd. (CT 47), Woodbury. Groomed trails with man-
made snow, night skiing, ski lodge, and equipment rentals.*

Northwest Park & Nature Center *(860-285-1886; www.north
westpark.org), 145 Lang Rd., Windsor. A mostly wooded 473-acre
municipal park with 12 miles of trails and lovely views of open meadows; equipment rentals are available.*

Denison Pequotsepos Nature Center *(860-536-1216;
www.dpnc.org), 109 Pequotsepos Rd., Mystic. Skiing in southern
Connecticut is hard to predict, but when snow blankets the ground this
300-acre wildlife sanctuary offers skiers 8 miles of trails through woodlands, wetlands, and meadows.*

* * * * * * * *

name suggests, a network of interlacing trails that can be linked in an
endless number of combinations, making it easy to spend the day in the
woods or return to the trailhead quickly, a plus for beginners or skiers
with young children in tow. Of the 42 trails—12.42 miles in all—about
half are for novices, the rest geared toward intermediate skiers and the
experts who fly through the woods during a weekly training series.
Twelve miles of trails are groomed daily, and there's snowmaking on a
2,000-foot loop, so unlike most other places in the state where you can
strap on your cross-country gear, if the snow disappears you don't have
to wait for it to snow again to hit the trails. It's also one of only three
cross-country ski centers in Connecticut that offer equipment rentals—
the ski shop is an official Rossignol demonstration center—and lessons
are led by certified instructors.

A good season sees upward of 30,000 skiers, which earns the smack-
in-the-suburbs facility a coveted spot in the top 1 percent of cross-country

ski areas in the nation. "We have our location to thank for that," Brown said. Weekends are particularly busy; after a decent snowfall, it's not uncommon to have a thousand skiers out on the trails.

As it turned out, we would be enjoying prime skiing conditions in March, thanks to a humdinger of a late-winter storm. And so it goes in southern New England, where winter and spring are known to switch roles and share the spotlight.

WINTER WONDERLAND

Cruising for Seals on Long Island Sound

For a growing number of outdoorsy types, summertime is passé. Who needs warmth, anyway? In Connecticut, cruising Long Island Sound in the deep chill of winter is more popular than ever. The draw? A chance to spot the migratory seals that take up residence in the chilly months. The perfect antidote, one could argue, to the midwinter blahs.

Certainly, there are easier ways to see these adorable creatures, but a bright and frozen Saturday morning finds me at the Maritime Aquarium at Norwalk, lured by the idea of a seal-watching trip aboard the 40-foot research vessel *Oceanic*. The Norwalk River was gray and icy as our group huddled on the aquarium's dock, all bundled up and filled with a mix of excitement and trepidation. Aquarium educator Cathy Hagadorn sized us up. "How many of you have been in a boat?" (all hands up). "How many of you have been in a boat in January in the North Atlantic?" (all hands down).

But there we were, lighting out in search of the seals that migrate into the Sound from as far north as Newfoundland. On select weekends, the public is invited along as aquarium researchers track the wintering seal population in the Norwalk Islands. Captain Art predicted smooth sailing, but the sunlit cabin was at the ready should the weather turn foul. There weren't many seals in residence yet, Hagadorn warned us, but our spirits

COURTESY OF THE MARITIME AQUARIUM

Lighthouse view: cruising the Norwalk Islands for wintering harbor seals

were buoyed just knowing they were out there. Our destination: the waters just beyond Sheffield Island, whose long stretch of rocks, known as the Great Reef, is a favorite pinniped gathering spot.

Out past the no-wake zone, a stiff wind blowing off the Sound was snapping the orange flags marking oyster beds and ruffling the feathers of sharp-tailed ducks, brant geese, and other wintering Arctic birds. Just past 11, right around low tide, Hagadorn told us to start looking for seals (harbor seals are the most common species at this latitude, but the larger gray seal is a regular visitor). As if on cue, someone let out a shriek that sent me fumbling for my binoculars. Captain Art swung the bow around to give us a better look, and there they were: a handful of sleek, brown harbor seals, bobbing in the waters off Sheffield Island.

The best views of the action were off port, where seven more harbor seals basked in the "banana" position, tails and heads arching toward the sky, leaving only their bellies touching the sun-baked rocks. We gaped in silent wonder as three others hauled out for a rest on a small upheaval known as Old Baldy, and nearly missed another dark, round head, slick as a scuba diver's, watching us from the waves sloshing around channel marker 283.

Abiding the 1972 Marine Mammal Protection Act, which lets these winter visitors go about their business with little disturbance, we give them a generous berth. But the most amazing portions of a seal's life happen far out of sight of tourists. The features that make seals so irresistible—big

---

IF YOU GO:

Winter Creature Cruises *(203-852-0700; www.maritimeaquarium .org), Maritime Aquarium at Norwalk, 10 North Water St., South Norwalk. Cruises operate on select weekends from December to early April; reservations are strongly recommended.*

The Maritime Aquarium at Norwalk *(203-852-0700; www. maritimeaquarium.org), 10 North Water St., South Norwalk. Open September through June daily 10–5; July and August daily 10–6; closed Thanksgiving and Christmas. Here, seven female harbor seals residing in a special indoor-outdoor tank get the full star treatment. The aquarium, which pulls in more than half a million visitors a year, is one of Connecticut's most popular tourist draws. The focus: more than a thousand marine animals indigenous to the Connecticut shore and Long Island Sound (others come just to see films at Connecticut's only IMAX theater).*

Getting there: *From I-95 take exit 15 southbound or exit 14 northbound. From the Merritt Parkway take exit 39A northbound or exit 40B southbound; follow US 7 south to South Norwalk.*

Winter basking

brown eyes, long whiskers, and potato-sack bodies—actually help them catch fish in dark water while staying under as long as 30 minutes.

Hagadorn nodded toward the island's 1868 stone lighthouse, a popular spot for summertime day-trippers. In the lantern room, a remote camera monitors the seals 24/7, channeling information to the aquarium's Harbor Seal Census Study. Researchers are studying, among other things, why the number of wintering seals is on the rise. While they are well adapted for swimming in frigid northern waters—kept warm by a layer of fat and a smooth heat-saving pelt—they migrate to southern New England for food (think crustaceans, squid, herring, cod) and find Connecticut's relatively mild coastal habitat and the Sound's brackish water much to their liking. Other factors include federal protection, ample fish stocks, and coastal development that's pushing seals farther from their pupping grounds in Maine and Canada.

We headed back toward terra firma in high spirits; the day's unofficial seal count was 16. Many were still on their way south, a journey of hundreds of miles that takes several weeks. "As long as they can still hunt and find fish up north, they'll still hang out up there," Hagadorn said.

Back on the river, Captain Art eased the *Oceanic* out of the main channel so researchers could complete a final check of the water's salinity and oxygen levels, and a somber back-to-reality mood settled on the boat as the aquarium's arching roofline came into view. We were treated to a side of Long Island Sound most people miss, but everyone promised to come back—next time in flip flops and shorts.

BEYOND HUSKYMANIA

The University of Connecticut at Storrs

Believe it or not, Husky fans, there *is* a university behind Connecticut's favorite basketball teams. The University of Connecticut's main campus is spread across 4,000 rural acres in the sleepy town of Storrs. What began as an agricultural college for boys in 1881 is now New England's top-ranked public university, with 28,000 students in 17 schools and colleges.

The men's and women's basketball teams are obsessions among Connecticut folks, many, interestingly enough, who have never stepped foot on campus. Pity, since it has much to offer, a treasure trove of American art and local artifacts, unusual plant specimens, and, of course, athletics; in all, a host of cultural riches for visitors who don't have a student in the family.

Read on, and plan your itinerary.

ART 101: THE WILLIAM BENTON MUSEUM OF ART

"I'm going to show you a photograph that I hope you'll remember your whole life," museum director Salvatore Scalora said as we gathered around a black-and-white image of a crying toddler whose mother was scavenging for food in an Indonesian trash dump.

We came to the William Benton Museum of Art—known simply as The Benton—for a tour of the Human Rights Gallery that's acclaimed for

All things Husky at the University of Connecticut at Storrs

its heavy-hitting topics; this time, children pressed into forced labor. We studied the images one by one: a Nepalese child chained to a loom; a nine-year-old Kenyan girl picking coffee beans; a teenage runaway-turned-prostitute in Mexico City.

The Benton, fresh off a $3.2 million redo, is a stylishly minimalist space whose glass facade lends it an urban storefront feel. While most of

❄ ❄ ❄ ❄ ❄ ❄ ❄ ❄

IF YOU GO:

University of Connecticut *(860-486-2000; athletic events: 860-486-5050; www.uconn.edu), CT 195, Storrs. Stop by Lodewick Visitors Center on Hillside Road for information or to take a student-led campus tour (reservations are required).*

William Benton Museum of Art *(860-486-4520; www.benton.uconn.edu), 245 Glenbrook Rd., Unit 2140. Open Tuesday through Friday 10–4:30, Saturday and Sunday 1–4:30; closed Monday. During the academic year open on Thursdays until 8 pm. Closed major holidays and school breaks.*

Husky Heritage Sports Museum *(860-486-8705), UConn Alumni Center, Alumni Dr. Open Monday through Friday 8–5, and two hours before the men's and women's basketball games at Gampel Pavilion.*

UConn Dairy Bar *(860-486-2634), 3636 Horsebarn Rd. Ext. Open daily year-round.*

University of Connecticut Greenhouses *(860-486-4052; www.eeb.uconn.edu), 75 North Eagleville Rd. Open Monday through Friday 8–4.*

Getting there: *Take exit 68 off I-84, then follow CT 195 to Storrs.*

❄ ❄ ❄ ❄ ❄ ❄ ❄ ❄

the galleries showcase the collection of 5,500 paintings, prints, drawings, sculptures, and photographs, the Human Rights Gallery is a catalyst for positive change: Awareness stirred by compassion, Scalora believes, leads, in turn, to action. "Numbers are meaningless," he said, "but when you see one photo, you connect."

HUSKY HOOPLA: THE HUSKY HERITAGE SPORTS MUSEUM

In the heart of winter, the hottest place to be on campus is the sidelines at Gampel Pavilion. If you can't score tickets to a Huskies basketball game, do the next best thing: Stop by the UConn Alumni Center, where an up-and-coming museum is devoted to all things Husky, including, of course, basketball.

The Huskies are the pride of Connecticut, so it may come as a surprise to learn the Husky Heritage Sports Museum is relatively new. The state-of-the-art space opened in 2002 with fascinating exhibits and a trove of memorabilia—*Sports Illustrated* covers, trophies, basketballs, jerseys, photos—loaned and donated by UConn alumni and fans. Visitors can watch games on a bank of television screens, and kids love the fiberglass statue of UConn's mascot, a white Siberian husky named Jonathan XII. The basketball Huskies generate big-time excitement in the Big East— during my visit, March Madness was at a fever pitch, and both teams were still in contention for the national title. But it's not all about basketball here: The history of UConn's intercollegiate athletic teams stretches back more than a century and includes soccer, football, rowing, and baseball, among many others.

SWEET TREATS: THE UCONN DAIRY BAR

Students, professors, and locals frequent this popular campus creamery, happily waiting in line for to-die-for creamy treats—in all, 25 flavors, including seasonal additions like pumpkin and cinnamon-caramel swirl, and the mascot-inspired Jonathan Supreme, which entails peanut butter sauce and chocolate-covered peanuts blended into vanilla ice cream.

The old-time 1950s-style soda fountain has been a campus

MORE UCONN

Connecticut State Museum of Natural History & Connecticut Archaeology Center *(860-486-4460; www.cac.uconn.edu), 2019 Hillside Rd. A must-see, especially if you've brought along youngsters.*

Jorgensen Center for the Performing Arts *(860-486-1904; ww.sfa.uconn.edu), 2132 Hillside Rd. UConn's art deco–style performance hall offers top-flight entertainment (think Tony Bennett, Wynton Marsalis, the Boston Pops).*

Ballard Institute and Museum of Puppetry *(860-486-4605; www.bimp.uconn.edu), UConn Depot Campus, 6 Bourn Place, Storrs. See the works of master puppeteer Frank Ballard and students in the Puppet Arts Program, the nation's first college degree program in puppetry.*

institution for half a century. Through the glass viewing window in the back of the shop, you just might spot Professor Dave Dzurek, crafting what loyal fans insist is the state's best ice cream. Afterward, visitors are welcome to take a self-guided tour of the animal barns on Horsebarn Hill.

PLANT IT AND THEY WILL COME: THE UNIVERSITY OF CONNECTICUT GREENHOUSES

Last, but often foremost on visitors' must-stop list, are UConn's internationally recognized Ecology and Evolutionary Biology Greenhouses, so named for their purpose: to nurture and study a diverse collection of plants from around the globe. With nearly 9,000 plants representing 2,500 species, something is always in bloom, from exotic orchids (900 varieties) to rare carnivorous plants. Visitors are welcome to wander about while students water, pot, and catalog plants (don't hesitate to ask them a question). It's easy to forget the blustery weather outside when surrounded in the greenhouses by exotic forms, scents, colors, and, thankfully, spring temperatures. The feathery fronds of a papyrus tree reach toward the sunlight, just yards from lush bougainvillea growing in bright fuchsia bursts, and bromeliads dripping with humidity.

And then there's *Amorphophallus titanum*—better known as the corpse plant. In 2004, some 22,000 people lined up for a glimpse, or a whiff, as it were, of its 10-foot-tall flower. "It's in bloom roughly one day out of every thousand," greenhouse manager Clint Morse said of the rare Sumatran specimen. "People waited more than an hour in line."

FLOWER POWER

The Connecticut Flower & Garden Show

L et's face it: By late winter, most of us have had enough deep freeze, and if there's anyone who thinks the season lasts too long, it's a gardener. Come February, restless green thumbs start to get a little antsy—too many short sunless days, too much abysmal weather, not enough warmth. We're hungry for green.

New England's top flower fests seem to arrive just in time, when my perennial beds in Litchfield are iron-hard and bare, "a view in India ink" as Dickens put it. The monochromatic color scheme and sharp etchings of bare branches, what horticulturalists call "winter interest," no longer interests me. I need color, and I need it now.

So on a particularly bleak February day—one punctuated by wet flurries, howling wind, and fog—I headed to Hartford for the Connecticut Flower & Garden Show, the state's premier gardening event. I was looking for spring, for warmth, and for blooms—lots and lots of blooms.

I didn't have to search long. The show of flowers just inside the door was extraordinary, a veritable oasis of daffodils, hyacinths, and tulips in their full cusp-of-spring glory. I filled my lungs with the heady scent of mulch and damp earth, and the sweet fragrance coming from row upon row of bulbs tricked me into thinking it was April. Beyond, purveyors of garden antiques, hard-to-find seeds, and every type of gizmo imaginable converged along with hibernating botanical types, armchair gardeners, and plantaholics united in a single affliction—cabin fever. "There's Daddy's favorite, paperwhites," a mother told her young son, who was crouching to inspect a box loaded with the ubiquitous bulbs that bloom indoors in winter. Nearby, two women were having an animated discussion over the best species for a native perennial bed. Others walked around clutching cheery cut flower bouquets, their free hands gesturing in every direction.

Indeed, there was a lot to point at. Gardeners need lots of stuff, and few things bring as much joy as great new ergonomically designed gadgets that make gardening chores a pleasure, from niceties (candy-striped Wellies, botanical art and jewelry) to necessities (trowels, bypass pruners, watering cans). Others come to flower shows for a sneak peek at the best new varieties of perennials, from no-brainer varieties for the brownest of thumbs, to exotic designer blooms that attract drive-by stares. I eyed a lush plumbago shrub, envisioning our overflowing shrub border and how I could squeeze one more in. "I simply *must* have that," a woman told her husband, nodding toward its tiny periwinkle blooms and unwittingly solving my dilemma.

The most idea-sparking settings were the display gardens created by professional landscape designers and local garden clubs; the theme, "Gardens of Zen and Now," was a nod to the Japanese-style gardens known for their soothing water elements like trickling streams and koi ponds. At the design and horticulture competition sponsored by the Federated Garden Clubs of Connecticut, arrangements ranged from funky to head-scratching, incorporating everything from ice skates and Slinky toys to climbing onions and Brazilian black lichen. In workshops and lectures, pros weighed in on an extensive variety of topics, giving budding gardeners answers to their green-thumb challenges. Garden guru and author Ken Druse encouraged us to plant trees and gardens not only for ourselves, but for future generations. "It doesn't matter if you'll be around to see them," he noted. "Someone will be around to see them."

I was ready to head home when a crowd huddled around a light-filled glass box caught my eye. Inside were dozens of flitting and fluttering

The Connecticut Flower & Garden Show is a harbinger of spring.

LAURA SOLL

butterflies and moths, courtesy of the Magic Wings butterfly conservatory in South Deerfield, Massachusetts. I spotted a pair of black and yellow striped zebra longwings, a stunning blue morpho, an orange Julia, a red and black piano keys, a pair of tiny moths with translucent wings, and an impossibly huge Atlas moth the size (I'm not kidding) of a small bird. In an instant, I realized what was so captivating—not the winged creatures themselves but their colors, a summery palette not seen in our New England landscape for months. And for a fleeting moment, although we couldn't feel the warmth or smell the flowers, it *was* summer.

On the way out, I braced myself against the soggy afternoon but took solace in a universal truth. It was all snow and chill outside, but a new gardening season was on the way. Soon, snowdrops and crocuses would poke out of the frozen earth, robins would be scratching in the soil, and so would I. While my arms were empty, my head was full of ideas and inspiration that warmed my cold winter mood. Ready to plunge headlong into spring, I wanted to go home and start more seeds than I'd ever be able to plant.

You can't hurry spring, but you can sure try.

❁ ❁ ❁ ❁ ❁ ❁ ❁ ❁

IF YOU GO:

The **Connecticut Flower & Garden Show** *(860-844-8461; www.ctflowershow.com), Connecticut Convention Center, Columbus Blvd., Hartford, is held over four days in February.* **Getting there:** *Take exit 29A off I-91.*

❁ ❁ ❁ ❁ ❁ ❁ ❁ ❁

Index